TRIUMPH
BONNEVILLE
PORTRAIT OF A LEGEND

JAMES MANN &
MICK DUCKWORTH

First published in March 2011

A catalogue record for this book is available from the British Library.

ISBN 978 0 85733 017 8

Library of Congress control no. 2010934900
Published by Haynes Publishing,
Sparkford, Yeovil, Somerset BA22 7JJ, UK.

Tel: 01963 442030 Fax: 01963 440001
Int. tel: +44 1963 442030
Int. fax: +44 1963 440001
E-mail: sales@haynes.co.uk
Website: www.haynes.co.uk

Haynes North America Inc.,
861 Lawrence Drive, Newbury Park,
California 91320, USA.

Design and page layout by Ryan Baptiste

Printed in the USA by Odcombe Press LP,
1299 Bridgestone Parkway, La Vergne, TN 37086

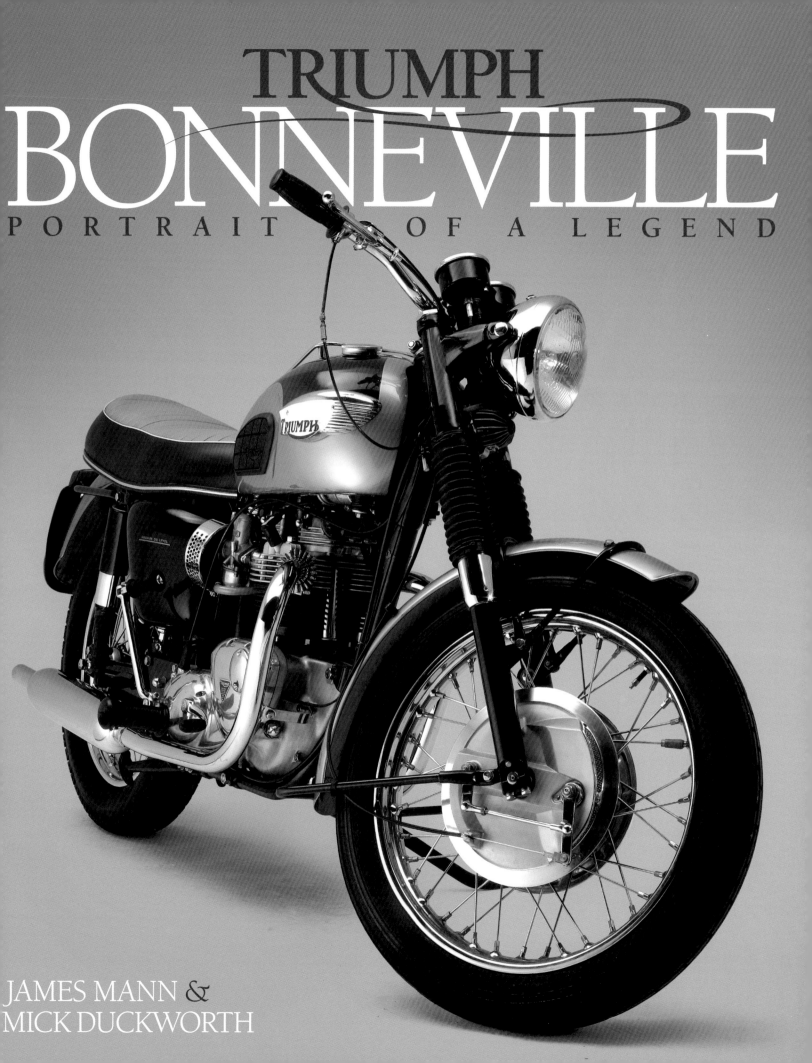

TRIUMPH
BONNEVILLE
PORTRAIT OF A LEGEND

JAMES MANN &
MICK DUCKWORTH

CONTENTS

The 1966 Bonneville T120C TT Special, a potent
competition machine for US off-road events.

INTRODUCTION

Britain's most famous motorcycle has one of the most enduring model names in automotive history. Born in a late-Fifties sales boom, the rip-snorting Triumph Bonneville grew to greatness and world fame through the Sixties. Narrowly surviving a devastating industry crisis in the early Seventies, the 'Bonnie' bounced back, albeit in more sedate form, to hang on for another few years before its apparent final demise in the Eighties.

By then, surviving machines from earlier decades had begun to be treasured and enthusiastic restorers of old Bonnevilles did their best to see that the legend did not fade. It didn't, for the Triumph Bonneville has returned in the 21st century to compete in a tough market and win through as a strong seller, delightful to ride and renowned for reliability.

When the original 650cc Bonneville was unveiled to the public at the end of 1958 it wasn't a revolutionary motorcycle, but the latest exciting development in a twin-cylinder line that Triumph had pursued for 20 years.

The brand had been founded by a German immigrant, Seigfried Bettman, at the end of the 19th century. He set up a cycle factory in Coventry, where a slump in the ribbon-making trade had left factory workers looking for jobs. Triumph progressed to motorcycle production in 1902 and its early products were speedy and rugged, as evidenced by the marque taking five out of the first ten places in the 1910 Isle of Man Tourist Trophy race. A few years later the 'Trusty Triumph' would prove its dependability as a standard-issue machine for First World War despatch riders.

By the mid-Thirties, Triumph's motor car was well established and the company decided to concentrate on four-wheelers. At that point Jack Sangster, whose family owned the Ariel motorcycle company, stepped in to rescue the Triumph two-wheeler. He made a deal to take over that side of the business, occupying Coventry premises that were being vacated. The new venture was called Triumph Engineering and Sangster brought in Ariel's dynamic young designer, Edward Turner, to take charge.

After designing the extraordinary Ariel Square Four engine for his previous employer, Turner was inspired to create a compact vertical twin unit. The result was the 500cc Triumph 5T Speed Twin, a sensation on its launch for 1938. The overhead valve twin's crisp throttle response and brisk 90mph-plus performance was a revelation to riders accustomed to thudding sports singles, while the price was set at an ultra-competitive £75.

Triumph Engineering's Coventry factory was destroyed by the Luftwaffe's nationwide blitz in November 1940. Fortunately the company was able to occupy a newly built plant outside the city, near the village of Meriden, in 1942. After a spat with Sangster, the mercurial Turner briefly moved to the rival BSA company, but was back in the fold by the end of the Second World War.

No time was lost in resuming civilian production at Triumph for 1946. Naturally the Speed Twin, now with telescopic fork front suspension, was the range leader. Its influence on the industry was such that within a very few years five other British manufacturers had introduced their own 500cc parallel twins.

All of UK industry was being urged to concentrate on exports to help a damaged and indebted nation recover and Triumph was exemplary in this regard, priority shipping to Commonwealth countries and many others. The real prize was the United States, where Edward Turner had appointed Johnson Motors of Pasadena, southern California as an official distributor in the Thirties. In 1951 a wholly owned subsidiary, the Triumph Corporation, opened near the Maryland port of Baltimore to serve the eastern states.

To American riders, a 500cc motorcycle was small potatoes, so Turner responded to requests for 'more cubes' by introducing a 100mph 650cc derivative of the 5T in 1950 and giving it the transatlantic-sounding name Thunderbird. Featured as Marlon Brando's ride in the 1953 Hollywood movie *The Wild One*, the rider-friendly Thunderbird would stay in the range until the Sixties, by which time it was a workhorse often seen pulling a sidecar on British roads.

Sangster sold Triumph Engineering to the Birmingham-based BSA group in 1951. The two heavyweight marques continued as salesroom rivals but a few years down the line in the mid-Sixties, when Turner took a back seat and management consultants McKinseys were brought in, pressure increased for greater unification between the two and catastrophe followed.

However, when the Bonneville was announced in the autumn of 1958, Triumph was in very robust shape. The British industry as a whole was headed for a production peak in excess of more than 234,000 units and the country's renowned high-performance motorcycles were in demand worldwide.

Although the Triumph twin is a quintessentially British motorcycle, its name comes from the famous speed venue in the American State of Utah. Bonneville Salt Flats is a dried-out lake named after Captain Benjamin Bonneville, a US Army officer and explorer of the American West in the 19th century.

It was there that in September 1956 Texan racer Johnny Allen set an absolute record speed for motorcycles at a fraction more than 214mph. He streaked across the salt inside a low-slung projectile powered by a radically tuned 650cc Triumph twin engine prepared by Jack Wilson, wizard mechanic at a Triumph dealership in Fort Worth. The cigar-like streamlined shell was the work of a fellow Texan, aviator J.H. 'Stormy' Mangham.

The Fédération Internationale Motocycliste (FIM) quibbled over a dubious technicality, so officially Triumph only had a national US record rather than a world record. But few cared about that, and in choosing the Bonneville name for 1959's new high-performance 650cc twin, Triumph cemented the association between the brand and extreme speed.

On the following pages a rich selection of Triumph Bonnevilles charts the model's long history, from cutting-edge roadburner of 1959 to modern classic of 2010. In the case of machines from the high-volume production years in the Sixties, it is worth noting that many of the updates described took place at various times during a season's build, rather than at the start of the year.

ACKNOWLEDGEMENTS

JAMES MANN

I'd like to thank a number of people who made this book happen. As ever Mark Hughes at Haynes, who always listens to my mad book concepts without even a hint of laughter. Mick Duckworth, who picked up the idea and ran with it, introducing me to most of the people who helped out at the Stafford Classic Motorcycle Show, including Roy Shilling of the Triumph Owners MCC who was very generous with his advice. And thanks. too, to all the owners listed below, many of whom rode their bikes to the various studios in Derby, London and Basingstoke and put up with my crazy schedule, some even arranging for friends and family to help out by transporting bikes by van through the rush hour to get the job done. And finally my family, who put up with me trying to juggle all the logistics and sort out the images late into the night.

MICK DUCKWORTH

Mick Duckworth wishes to thanks the following for their help: Ace Classics, Bill Crosby, BS Bikes, Hugh Dickson, John Birch at LF Harris International, John Hallard at Meriden Motorcycles, John Healy at Coventry Spares (USA), John Nelson, John Rosamond, Lindsay Brooke, Triumph Motorcycles Limited and the Vintage Motor Cycle Club Library.

THE FEATURED BIKES

1954 Tiger 110	Keith Reed
1959 T120 US	Ace Classics (Cliff Rushworth)
1959 T120 US	Ace Classics
1960 T120	Ace Classics
1961 T120	Ace Classics
1962 T120R US	Ace Classics
1963 T120 US	Ace Classics
1965 T120C US	Graham Bowen
1965 Thruxton T120	Geoff Parker
1966 T120R US	Ace Classics
1968 T120 R	Graham Bowen
1968 T120 UK	The Bike Shed (Hugh Brown)
1969 T120R US	Graham Bowen
1966 T120TT US	Graham Bowen
1970 T120R/T	Graham Bowen
1972 T120 UK Show Special	Will Holder
1977 T140J Silver Jubilee UK	Ray Twiss
1982 T140LE Royal Wedding US	Andrew Ball
1983 TSS-AV	Erum Waheed
1983 TSX	Erum Waheed
1988 T140LF Harris	David Drew
2010 Bonneville Sixty	Metropolis Motorcycles, London (Tony Woodall)

1954 TIGER 110

Fastest machine in Triumph's range from
1954 to 1958, the Tiger 110 has a style that
is both elegant and purposeful. A Tiger-like
snarl comes from the twin silencers when
the throttle is wound open.

Carrying the right connotations of litheness and ferocity, the Tiger model name was adopted by Triumph for Edward Turner-designed sports singles launched in 1936. The 500cc version was the Tiger 90 with the implication that the number referred to maximum speed. A tuned version of the 500cc Speed Twin launched in 1939 nicely filled the Tiger 100 slot. After Triumph introduced its 650cc engine on the 1950 6T Thunderbird, the next step was a high-performance version worthy to be called the Tiger 110.

Truly Tigerish in character, the fastest Triumph to date reached the market in 1954, the first year of Triumph's swinging-arm frame. After several years of offering its patent sprung-hub rear suspension, Triumph accepted that a pivoted arm with twin shock absorbers was superior. The design is not perfect, tending to cause weaves when cornering at speed, especially if a rider loses nerve and eases the throttle.

The 650cc engine's bottom end had been beefed up with a larger timing-side main bearing and tuning for the T110 included higher-compression pistons, hotter cams and a new cast-iron cylinder head, identifiable by five horizontal fins where the 6T had four. To cope with the performance, an 8in-diameter front drum brake was specified, with a scoop for cooling air on its backplate.

While the Thunderbird acquired coil ignition, the T110 had a

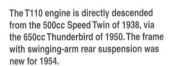

The T110 engine is directly descended from the 500cc Speed Twin of 1938, via the 650cc Thunderbird of 1950. The frame with swinging-arm rear suspension was new for 1954.

magneto with a handlebar lever to alter spark timing. Full advance was used on the open road, while retarding softened the engine for slow riding.

Styling was in the same vein as the Thunderbird, with the nacelled headlamp introduced on the first six-fifty. While conservative, designs conceived in the early Fifties by Edward Turner and executed by Meriden's chief stylist, Jack Wickes, possessed a symmetry and grace that few other motorcycle makers matched.

The fuel tank embellishments with a Triumph logo and four horizontal bars were not merely elegant: Turner devised them to cut the cost of producing tanks with more conventional all-over chromium plate. A shallow dual seat and slightly tilted-up silencers underline the Tiger's sporting character.

Shell Blue paint on the tank and mudguards was shared with the model's smaller brother, the 500cc Tiger 100. Triumph generally favoured darker colours in the early Fifties, but had rapidly dropped the blue-grey chosen for the first year of the Thunderbird in 1950. US riders thought it too sombre and Australian dealers were horrified: a similar shade

Triumph twins have a slim frontal profile despite the parallel cylinders. A narrow front tyre with a ribbed tread was normal wear for a Fifties' sports machine.

of paint was widely used to identify public lavatories in that country, where the 6T earned a distasteful nickname.

Press tests of the Tiger 110 confirmed that owners could expect 110mph – and possibly more. The weekly *Motor Cycling* assessed the mainly-for-export model late in 1954 and quoted maximum speed as 113mph, while a flash reading of 117mph was reported after fitting a larger main jet (220 in place of 200).

Factories were not beyond performance-tweaking press test machines, but even so the snarling T110 was the most exciting motorcycle you could buy, with the possible exception of the much more expensive 1,000cc Vincent V-twin made in smaller quantities. Yet the single carburettor six-fifty was a versatile machine that was quite manageable in town traffic.

Known as the 'Ton Ten' to British bikers and called the 'Tiger-Bird' in America, the fastest Triumph was modernised for 1956 with an attractive aluminium alloy cylinder head. Lighter than the previous iron component, the 'Delta head' also ran cooler and could cope with higher compression ratios. Incorporating internal oil drainage to replace the external copper pipes on the iron head, the casting had to be strengthened after the first year to avoid cracking between the valve seats and fixing bolts.

A head of similar appearance was catalogued as a high-performance extra for the Tiger 100 in 1957, with intake stubs to accept twin carburettors and bigger inlet valves. Aimed at American tuners, both professional and amateur, it whetted their appetites for an equivalent 650cc head. By 1958 such an item was listed as a performance part in the US, where demand proved overwhelming and Triumph dealers were increasingly being asked when a stock twin-carb six-fifty would be available.

That happened in 1959, and the Tiger 110 then assumed a sports tourer role, fitted in 1960 with the rear wheel enclosure that Turner was keen on. He liked to call it streamlining and was apparently miffed when it was deemed inappropriate for the Bonneville.

The 1954 Tiger 110 seen here was restored by Ace Classics for lifelong Triumph rider Keith Reed of Erith, Kent.

The headlamp nacelle, 1in-diameter handlebars and tank-top parcel grid were Triumph trademarks. Note the unusual speedometer dial with calibrations to show rpm in the four gears.

Right: The cast-iron cylinder head is topped by separate rocker boxes, each with two screw-caps that are removed to check valve clearances. Finned clamps secure the exhaust pipes to stubs in the head.

Right: A six-volt dynamo to power the electrical system mounts at the front of the crankcase.

Far right: Oil for the dry sump lubrication system is carried in a tank on the right side of the machine, under the seat.

Left: The Amal Type 289 carburettor has main and reserve feeds from the tank. A 'tickler' button on the float chamber top is depressed to flood the instrument for cold starting. An external oil drain from the rocker box is at the rear of the cylinder.

1954 Tiger 110 specifications	
Cubic capacity	649cc (71x82mm)
Compression ratio	8.5:1
Carburation	1 1/8in Amal 289
Ignition	Lucas magneto
Max power	42bhp @ 6,500rpm
Gearbox	Four-speed
Wheels	Front 19in, rear 19in
Brakes	Front 8in drum, rear 7in drum
Fuel capacity	4 gal
Weight	395lb (179kg)

Above: Dual seats replaced separate saddles and pillion pads in the early Fifties.

Left: The front brake's air-scoop is protected from foreign bodies by steel gauze.

1959
T120
US (EARLY)

Strange as it may seem today, the Bonneville legend didn't begin with a big bang. Press and publicity leading up to the 1958 Earls Court Show focused on an all-new 500cc Triumph Speed Twin rather than the latest six-fifty. The modernised five-hundred was expected to go down well on the home market, while the bigger twin was mainly for US export. From the first 1959 build, more than 1,100 would go to the US against fewer than 800 for all other markets.

But when show time came, Triumph's new range leader, resplendent in Tangerine and Pearl Grey, was a focus of admiration. A T120 model code suggesting a breathtaking 'ton-twenty' maximum could not fail to excite, yet the new Triumph twin had a reassuring pedigree, being ostensibly a Tiger 110 in fresh paint with a new cylinder head showing off the twin carburettors to advantage.

The lineage went back even further, to Edward Turner's revolutionary Speed Twin: the T120 engine closely follows the original Thirties' layout.

The two pistons rise and fall together on a 360-degree crankshaft in parallel bores. The cylinders fire on alternate strokes, producing a power impulse for every complete turn of the crankshaft. Supported in two main bearings, the shaft has a central flywheel between the crankpins, on which plain big-end bearings carry high-strength aluminium connecting rods.

Individual inlet and exhaust camshafts in the upper crankcase are driven by gears from the

The first Bonneville was rushed onto the market for 1959, wearing distinctive Pearl Grey and Tangerine paint. High handlebars identify this as a US export.

crankshaft. They operate the two valves in each cylinder via pushrods enclosed in distinctive chromium-plated tubes outside the one-piece iron cylinder block. The cylinder head, cast iron on earlier Triumph twins but in aluminium on all Bonnevilles, is a single casting with hemispherical combustion chambers. Two separate aluminium rocker boxes bolt down on top of the head and there is a 90-degree included angle between the inlet and exhaust valves. The spark plugs are accessibly placed on each side of the head. Slightly outward-facing exhaust ports give the exhaust down-pipes a pleasing line, to complement the symmetry of the upper engine.

Simple and inexpensive to manufacture, easy to maintain and rewardingly responsive to conventional tuning, the classic Triumph twin engine also possessed a certain style and a distinctive brand identity. Its main drawback was the inherent lack of balance of the crankshaft layout, causing vibration. During the Bonneville's long production life engineers would do all they could to minimise the vibes, but they couldn't be eliminated. It wasn't considered a serious problem until super-smooth motorcycle engines arrived in the Seventies,

A leaping Tiger motif, designed for Triumph in the US by a Disney Studios artist, beautifies the unused front number plate.

and even then – for some Triumph customers – being able to feel the engine was the sign of a 'real man's machine'.

Visible cycle part differences from the T110 on the previous pages include a deeper front mudguard and new style of tank badge. Inspired by the grilles and bumpers of glamorous sports cars, the new emblem was introduced, along with fashionable two-tone paint, in 1957. It was destined to become a widely recognised icon, even worn as a belt buckle by the more showily dressed of Sixties' rockers.

Raised handlebars, anathema to the European sports rider who liked a lower 'bar for comfortable cruising at speed, were specific to American-market machines while the tiger motif on the number plate was a common decoration in the US, where only a rear licence plate was required.

The Bonneville's genesis was in the Meriden factory's experimental department, run by Frank Baker. Twin-carburettor 500cc Triumph twins had been around for years and it was only logical to convert a Tiger 110 engine. The department's test rider and

noted road racer Percy Tait put Baker's experimental 650cc motor through its paces at the Motor Industries Research Association (MIRA) proving grounds. Timed at 128mph, it was far faster than anything on the market but plagued by carburation trouble at high rpm, when engine vibration caused frothing in the float chambers. Amal, Britain's only maker of carburettors for high-performance motorcycles, helped out with a flexibly mounted remote float chamber (often used with racing carburettors) and supplied Monobloc instruments with

machined-off float chambers.

The existing three-piece 650cc crankshaft was replaced by a stronger one-piece item with the flywheel ring bolted to the periphery of its centre section.

As the launch of a production twin-carburettor six-fifty grew closer, the unpredictable Turner openly expressed doubts over its wisdom. But he was aware that BSA listed the 110mph 650cc Super Rocket for 1958 and a twin-carburettor 600cc Norton Dominator sports machine was imminent. Triumph's claims of superior speed had to be backed up.

The button on top of the nacelle is an engine cut-out.

The T120 cylinder head has stubs to hold the carburettors, threaded into the casting and locked with hexagon nuts. Screws on the machined-off float chambers are locked with wire to prevent loosening.

The Lucas K2F competition magneto has red high-tension pick-ups for the yellow and black plug leads. The ignition cut-out terminal is on the end cap.

Chrome tank badges are in the style introduced for 1957 and rubber knee-grips fit over screw-on carrier plates. The parcel rack remains, even on a model built for speeding rather than shopping.

TRIUMPH

Bonneville 120

A combined headlamp dip-switch and horn push are mounted on the left handlebar for thumb operation.

Deep mudguarding made sense for all-weather
riders but did not appeal to Californian customers.

1959 T120 US (early) specifications	
Cubic capacity	649cc (71x82mm)
Compression ratio	8.5:1
Carburation	Two 1 1/16in Amal Monobloc
Ignition	Lucas magneto
Charging system	6v dynamo
Max power	46bhp @ 6,500rpm
Gearbox	Four-speed
Wheels	Front 19in, rear 19in
Brakes	Front 8in, rear 7in
Fuel capacity	3 gal
Weight	404lb (183kg)

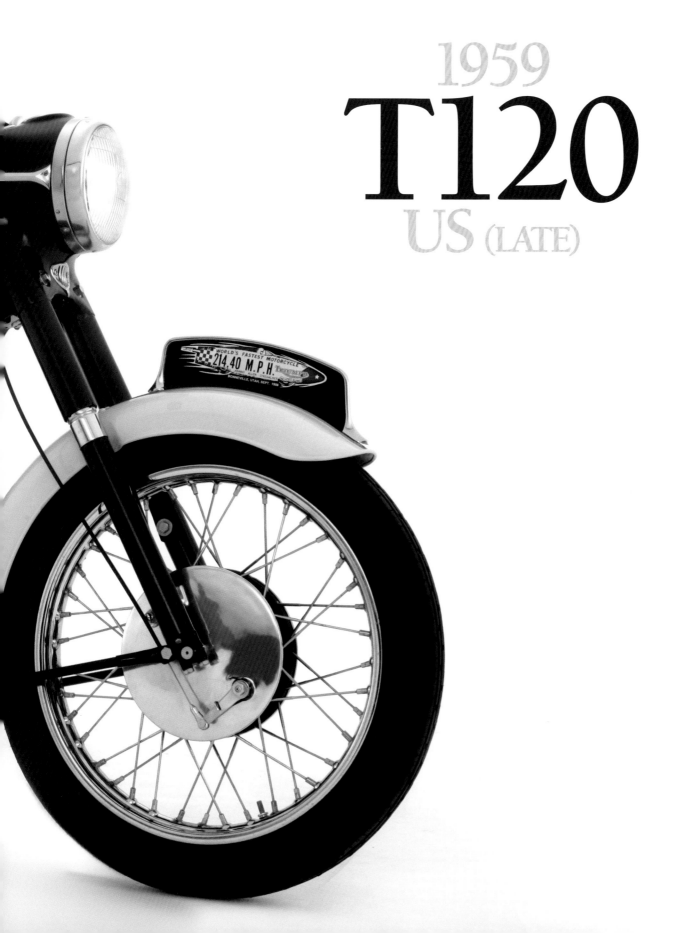

1959
T120
US (LATE)

This is a 1959 US market T120 wearing the revised two-tone colour scheme that was introduced before the year's production ended and retained for the 1960 build. Former Tangerine areas are now Royal Blue, while the Pearl Grey remains as before. The change may have been due to an unfavourable reaction to the original colours.

Like the earlier 1959 model and several others on these pages, this machine was restored by Ace Classics. The south London shop has for many years concentrated on Fifties' and early Sixties' 650cc Triumph twins, buying up genuine Meriden parts and organising the manufacture of high-quality replica components where necessary.

Not everything is exactly as it

would have been when the bike left the factory. For example, it has a rocking 'heel and toe' gear-shift pedal that was a popular fitment, marketed in the US as a genuine accessory with a Triumph part number. The T120's constant-mesh gearbox has its mainshaft

set above the layshaft with output at the mainshaft, inboard of the clutch. Gear selection is with forks motivated by a cam-plate mounted at 90 degrees to the shafts and operated from the foot lever by a positive-stop quadrant mechanism. Primary drive is by chain to a

By the time 1959's production run ended, Tangerine paint had been replaced by Royal Blue. The front number plate on this US-market machine celebrates Triumph's 1956 214mph speed record.

multi-plate clutch in an oil bath. From 1958 to 1961, Triumph fitted 650cc twin gear pedals with a Slickshift mechanism to ease the clutch whenever the gear lever was operated. Experienced riders were unenthusiastic and it was not specified for the Bonneville.

This engine has another option available to US owners: a timing cover incorporating a rev-counter drive taken off the exhaust camshaft, and a Smiths Chronometric instrument clamped to the left handlebar. When the headlamp nacelle was discontinued for 1960, the rev-counter and speedometer could be mounted side by side, a much neater arrangement. Even if not strictly necessary for road riding, a rev-counter was considered a desirable fitment for a machine like the Bonneville, which was all about high performance.

The oil-feed pipes and banjo unions supplying the valve rockers have been replaced by a Monard finned alloy item, marketed by British tuning shop Monty & Ward. Typical of 'bolt-on goodies' that were popular to the point of a craze in the Sixties, it is stronger than the copper pipes and probably helps oil cooling – and it looks neat. The oil feed to the upper engine is taken off the dry-sump system's return line from the engine to the oil tank. A double-plunger oil pump, a type favoured by Triumph since the Thirties and used with various modifications throughout Meriden Bonneville production, is driven off the inlet

camshaft's drive pinion by a peg and sliding block arrangement.

Triumph was unusual among British makers in fitting 1in (25.5mm) diameter handlebars when 7/8in (21mm) had become the norm. All 650cc twins eventually acquired the slimmer tubing in 1963. Although Meriden took the trouble to fit raised handlebars to suit American preference, the chosen pattern was not always well received and John Healy, a long-time Triumph dealer in Boston, Massachusetts, recalls that it took the best part of ten years to persuade Meriden to fit the form of 'bars his customers liked. It was not unusual for US dealers to change them for an aftermarket type before selling a new machine and one company in particular, California-based Flanders Inc., offered a huge choice of bends.

From the start of production ball-ended brake and clutch levers, compulsory in competitions for safety reasons, were fitted.

Early Bonnevilles were advertised as being selectively assembled and individually bench-tested at the factory, emphasising that it

Above: The front mudguard's lower stay can be dropped down for use as a wheel stand.

Right: The rev-counter head clamped to the handlebar was one of a number of accessories listed by Triumph US distributors.

was a specialist speed model. In later years, production output would rise so dramatically that such detailed attention would be impossible. Until Triumph had a rolling road installed in 1966, a team of production testers would ride machines fresh off the assembly line, fitted with temporary fuel tanks and exhausts. Their normal route went through the village of Meriden and down a mile-long straight towards Hampton-in-Arden. Machines were checked over, minor adjustments made to them if necessary and then ridden back to the factory, where clean tanks and pipes were fitted ready for despatch. Meriden service department chief John Nelson recalls that the US Department of Agriculture wanted the practice stopped, because imported machines contaminated by road dirt might carry livestock or crop diseases.

The 'World's Fastest Motorcycle' decals seen on a front number plate that would otherwise be blank in the US are copied from originals celebrating Triumph's 1956 Bonneville record.

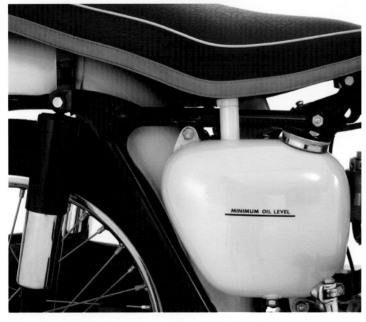

The single float chamber is suspended between the carburettor bodies. A finned rocker box oil feed has been added to this engine. The transfer on the oil tank indicates the correct level.

This machine carries a rocking-pedal gear change available to US buyers. A special timing cover provides drive for the rev-counter off the exhaust camshaft.

The parcel grid has been removed from this fuel tank and small flexible bungs, available as a spare, used to fill the threaded holes.

The lever on the throttle side of the
handlebars is for manual adjustment of
ignition timing. Triumph changed to auto-
advancing to minimise service issues.

1959 T120 US (late) specifications

Cubic capacity	649cc (71x82mm)
Compression ratio	8.5:1
Carburation	Two Amal 1 1/16in Monobloc
Ignition	Lucas dynamo
Charging system	6v alternator
Max power	48bhp @ 6,750rpm
Gearbox	Four-speed
Wheels	Front 19in, rear 19in
Brakes	Front 8in drum, rear 7in drum
Fuel capacity	4 gal
Weight	404lb (183kg)

Above: An eye in the frame below the seat nose is provided for sidecar attachment. The frame was shared with the Thunderbird tourer.

1960
T120
UK & GENERAL EXPORT

Triumph made major changes to Bonneville after only one year of production. While there were few internal differences and the late-1959 Royal Blue/Pearl Grey colour scheme was still applied, the second-season 1960 model looks substantially different from the first T120.

The Tiger 110 styling of the first Bonneville had received a cool reception from American dealers and riders not expecting Triumph's hot new 120mph machine to come with a headlamp nacelle and deep fenders, suggesting a sedate and sensible tourer. Johnson Motors were particularly vexed by the T120's lack of visual panache as the rival BSA brand had out-sold Triumph in western states during 1959.

A new frame was adopted for all three 650cc models (Bonneville, Tiger 110 and Thunderbird) for 1960. As can be seen, it features twin downtubes that continue under the engine and gearbox. The upper frame has a single larger-diameter tube running from the forged steering head to a point under the seat nose, where it joins a vertical tube running down to a malleable iron cross-member connecting to the engine cradle. A hefty lug to support the swinging-arm pivot is carried on the vertical tube. During production an extra tube was added, running from a bridging piece on the downtubes a couple of inches below the steering head back to a point on the top tube just ahead of the seat's front mounting lugs. The strengthening was in response to reports of excessive vibration and, more seriously, breakages near the steering head on T120s and

TR6 Trophies used in American off-road sport.

The bolted-up rear subframe has a full loop supporting the seat, with upper mounts for the rear suspension placed where tubes running up from the bottom forging terminate. The entire assembly was hearth-brazed in the traditional Meriden way.

The 1960 front fork has improved spring and damping action, to ride better over small bumps and expansion joints, and the frame revisions saw the steering-head angle made a few degrees shallower.

Other more cosmetic changes to create the leaner, more purposeful look include replacing the nacelle with a discrete chrome-plated 7in headlamp and separate speedometer. Flexible fork gaiters in place of steel shrouds and shallower mudguards complete the sportier lines.

In effect the T120 was made to look more like the single-carburettor 650cc TR6 Trophy, a big hit with off-road sport riders since the mid-Fifties. To emphasise the connection, for marketing purposes the 1960 Bonneville was coded TR7 in the

Heavily revised cycle parts for 1960 include a twin-downtube frame, separate headlamp with chromed shell and lighter mudguarding. Low-set handlebars on the UK version suit high-speed riding.

US, rather than T120. A TR7/B scrambler version was introduced to compete with BSA's single-cylinder 500cc Catalina Scrambler, which was responsible for much of that marque's sales boom in California.

The Lucas dynamo was replaced by a theoretically more reliable six-volt AC alternator of the same make, mounted at the drive end of the crankshaft as it had been on the Thunderbird since 1954. However, while the 6T had alternator-powered coil ignition, the magneto preferred by most sporting riders was retained although manual timing adjustment was replaced by an auto-advance unit on UK machines. While the coil system usually gives better starting, a magneto produces a stronger spark the faster it turns. Export machines were usually equipped with the Lucas K2FR high-specification competition instrument known as the 'red label' after the colour of its makers' plate. Today's restorers buy a red plate to rivet on for an easy but ineffective upgrade.

Among the few other engine alterations was a better method of suspending the carburettors' remote float bowl, now hung on a rod fixed in a flexible bush attached to the engine's head-steady plate. The rod is threaded so nuts can be turned on it to adjust float height, critical for maximum performance from the Amal Monobloc instruments, still with truncated float chambers.

The early history of this particular Bonneville is known. Bought new by south Londoner Ernie Parrish, it was an outstandingly fast example. Cruising the suburbs on a Sunday morning, Ernie would challenge other riders in a burn-up and usually blow them off. As was usual in the Sixties, he modified his bike with low clip-on handlebars and a large fuel tank, calling it the EP Special. The next owner was Brian Clarke who sold it when he married in 1964. Decades later, Cliff Rushworth of Ace Classics bought YLN 556 rough, but running, in Eltham as a restoration project. A friend of Brian's was at the shop, recognised the registration and a reunion was arranged. To date Ernie, the fastest Bonnie rider in the South (to paraphrase Benny Hill), has not been traced.

Removing the nacelle makes room for mounting the speedometer and rev-counter together on a steel bracket. The knob in front of them tightens the friction-type steering damper.

Identification. The model code is always stamped on the crankcase and from 1960 serial numbers have a letter prefix.

The chrome embellishment plate on the full-width front hub no longer has the radial pattern seen on 1959 machines.

A re-shaped primary chaincase accommodates the alternator. The outer case is retained by cross-head screws which were often replaced by aftermarket cap-head types. A spanner from the tool kit fits the slot in the oil filler cap.

A rubber-backed steel strap holds the fuel tank in place on the duplex frame. Three rubber buffers support it from below.

Flexible fork gaiters were first fitted in 1960.

The larger fuel tank on non-US machines
has a different shape of rubber knee grip.

1960 T120 UK & General Export specifications

Cubic capacity	649cc (71x82mm)
Compression ratio	8.5:1
Carburation	Two 1 1/16in Amal Monobloc
Ignition	Lucas magneto
Max power	46bhp @ 6,500rpm
Gearbox	Four-speed
Wheels	Front 19in, rear 19in
Brakes	Front 8in drum, rear 7in drum
Fuel capacity	4 gal
Weight	393lb (178kg)

1961
T120
UK & GENERAL EXPORT

David Dixon, road tester for *The Motor Cycle*, had a new-model Sky Blue and silver Bonneville for several mainly wet days at the end of 1960 and rated it highly, for its tractability as much as the top-end performance, describing the joy of accelerating from 80mph to 105mph in top gear. 'An absolute honey' was his verdict.

Midway through the year, the weekly magazine *Motor Cycling*

tested the 1961 Bonneville in better conditions, reporting that it lapped the MIRA banked circuit at 108mph and made a one-way run at 115mph with the rider prone and in a slight tailwind.

In that year's Thruxton 500-mile race for standard production machines a Bonneville shared by Tony Godfrey and John Holder took the overall win, after close tussles with Norton and Velocette rivals. The dealer-entered Triumph

completed 220 laps of the bumpy former airfield circuit, averaging just over 67mph for seven and a half hours, the first three of them in rain.

Even if they couldn't afford a new Bonneville, many of Britain's growing number of young riders, sometimes scornfully called coffee-bar cowboys, looked to Triumph's range-topper as the ultimate 'ton-up' tool. In their eyes, having only a single carburettor militated

against BSA's otherwise fine 650cc Super Rocket, and Norton's Dominator twins, though fast and with superb handling, were expensive to buy and spares back-up was weak.

Apart from paint colours and two complete carburettors replacing the remote float arrangement, the Bonneville's updates were not highly visible. Rear wheel rim size was reduced from 19in to 18in and an improvement was made

New colours and vertical stays cast into the cylinder head finning to prevent ringing noise are among few changes from 1960. The plated cover on the gearbox just behind the rider's footrest is carried over from other 650cc twins with the Slickshift mechanism.

MINIMUM OIL LEVEL

to braking. In the front drum the shoes were allowed to float on the pivot opposite the operating cam, allowing better contact with the drum surface.

The Smiths Chronometric speedometer was calibrated to 140mph instead of 120mph and the rev-counter casing was now illuminated when the lights were on.

A combination of engine vibration and skimping on quality meant that electrical component failure was a major annoyance for riders buying new Bonnevilles.

The thrilling performance was marred by irritating faults such as misfires, cracked batteries and potentially lethal lighting failures. The Lucas brand's 'King of the Road' slogan was often sarcastically re-worded to 'Prince of Darkness'. Triumph, who stood to lose business, put pressure on the vehicle electrical specialist to do better but was not always prepared to pay more for the equipment.

Rocker box caps were often loosened by vibration. Titch Allen, founder of the Vintage Motor Cycle Club, once said that at one time

there must have been thousands lying in the grass verges of Britain's roads. Jack Mercer of the Triumph Corporation in America joked that he was able to put his kids through college on the takings from replacement caps.

Despite these foibles Triumph was poised to go from strength to strength across the Atlantic. Tri-Cor, distributing in 31 eastern and southern states, was building a highly effective network of large and small dealers. Travelling representatives or 'road men' made regular visits to gain feedback and encourage improvements to premises, fostering a 'Triumph family' atmosphere. Eastern and mid-western industrial states such as Illinois, New Jersey, Michigan, Ohio and Pennsylvania became prime Triumph territory.

Johnson Motors, which remained independent until being bought out by BSA in 1965, had more spread-out dealers in less populous western states to cater for, as well as the teeming urban areas around San Francisco and Los Angeles, the latter having an ideal climate for motorcycling. Links with Hollywood and star names like Steve McQueen and Clint Eastwood reinforced the glamorous image of Triumph twins. The brand image was cool and sometimes perceived as being just as American as the famous Milwaukee marque.

When Honda ventured into the US market in the early Sixties, Triumph's methods were closely studied. Within a few years, Triumph dealers were encouraged to stock both makes, as riders starting out on Japanese lightweights often bought British products when they moved up to big bikes. Meriden even had to punch holes in parts book pages to suit Honda's posh swivelling lecterns.

While the US market was set to explode, motorcycling faced setbacks in Britain. Unlike Americans, UK riders had traditionally bought motorcycles as much for transport as recreation. Once small, affordable cars like the Ford Popular and the milestone Austin and Morris Minis of 1959 came along, customers were being seduced by the comfort and shelter they offered. And although ton-up boys and rockers had a lot of fun, they didn't exactly enhance the public image of motorcycling.

The speedometer's upper range was extended from 120mph to 140mph, a subtle sales aid.

Exhaust pipe run on the left is slightly lower, to run below primary chaincase.

Bosses that rest on anti-vibration rubbers are built into the nose of the fuel tank. Front number plates were mandatory in the UK until 1975.

MINIMUM OIL LEVEL

TRIUMPH

AMAL
MADE IN
ENGLAND

Above: A transfer conveniently displays valve
clearance figures on the forward engine mounting

Left: The Monobloc carburettors with complete float
chambers still have locking wire on their end-cover screws.

A butterfly nut at the end of the rear brake operating rod makes adjustment quick and easy. It usually needs re-setting after the drive chain is adjusted.

1961 T120 UK & General Export specifications

Cubic capacity	649cc (71x82mm)
Compression ratio	8.5:1
Carburation	Two Amal 1 1/16in Monobloc
Ignition	Lucas magneto
Charging system	6v alternator
Max power	46bhp @ 6,500rpm
Gearbox	Four-speed
Wheels	Front 19in, rear 18in
Brakes	Front 8in drum, rear 7in sls drum
Fuel capacity	4 gal
Weight	395lb (166kg)

1962 T120R US

A real stunner in Flamboyant Flame and silver, this is the US-export Bonneville of 1962 in the T120C variant's off-road trim, wearing upswept exhaust pipes for increased ground clearance and a 'bash plate' under the front of the engine to protect against impact from rocks or tree stumps. However, the Avon road tyres show that this is not so much a desert racer or forest trail-blazer as a street scrambler.

Triumph had long catered for America's off-road sporting riders, its first purpose-built competition machines being the single-carburettor 500cc TR5 and 650cc TR6 Trophy twins first exported in the Fifties. They were largely based on specifications devised for Meriden's successful forays in the International Six Days Trial, where high speeds had to be maintained over a variety of terrain in all weathers. Launched for 1956, the bigger TR6 Trophy-Bird soon gained a reputation as the top gun in western states' desert races that attracted entries by the hundred. Competitors stripped lights and other road equipment off their TR6s to create what they called 'desert sleds'.

When the Bonneville came along it promised more horsepower for top-notch off-roaders who could handle it – and the less skilled who thought they could handle it. Encouraged by western distributor Johnson Motors, Meriden introduced the Bonneville

Scrambler for 1960. In its first year, it was marketed as the Triumph TR7/B to align it with the 1960 TR6/B, but was subsequently coded as the T120C.

But it was not only serious competition riders who appreciated the 'C models'. As had happened with the Trophy, tarmac riders across the US were attracted by their purposeful looks. Cool rides for downtown boulevards, suburban byways or the open highway, high-piped Triumphs were

pioneers of the street scrambler style that is still in favour today.

Tractability is vital for off-roading and in 1962 all T120s were fitted with heavier crankshaft flywheels to help in this direction. To reduce vibration the crank balance factor was shifted from 50 per cent to just above 70 per cent, until a new crankshaft assembly with an 85 per cent factor was introduced during 1962 production. To prevent cracking of the oil tank's mountings, it was isolated from

vibration by rubber bushes at its fixing points.

The wiring socket provided for rapid headlamp removal was discontinued during the 1962 model year. Its tendency to disconnect itself on the move was a serious safety hazard and street riders did not need the facility. Pure off-road T120Cs without lights were in the pipeline.

The Monobloc carburettors still had yawning open bell-mouths that allowed damaging particles to enter

Street scrambler! The high-level exhaust pipes have slotted heat shields above the footrests to protect the rider's legs.

A quick-release plug and socket connection for the headlamp is retained on C models, but was dropped on road machines during 1962.

the engine, especially in dry and dusty desert conditions: Triumph would start fitting filters in 1963. Road racer-style locking wire is used to prevent the float bowl end-cover screws from loosening.

A notable detail on this machine is the gold background for black Triumph lettering on the tank badges in place of the previous black on white. Such details can be confusing for restorers seeking perfection. The front number plate blade carries a leaping tiger motif commonly applied to Triumphs in America since the Fifties. Home-market Bonnevilles for 1961 stuck

with the previous year's more restrained blue and silver scheme.

A pillion rider's grab-strap can be seen on this machine, fixed to the sides of the seat base by swivelling metal loops. Triumph was forced to fit them to machines destined for Johnson Motors as they were mandatory under Californian highway regulations. To simplify manufacture, all seat bases had provision for the strap but only those destined for the West Coast were fitted with it.

An important milestone in Triumph history occurred at Bonneville Salt Flats in 1962 when

a rocket-like Triumph-powered streamliner piloted by Bill Johnson (not related to the boss of Johnson Motors) set an FIM-sanctioned absolute motorcycle world speed record at 224.57mph, averaged from runs in two directions. The national AMA body recognised a one-way flying-mile record at 230.269mph.

Johnson's vehicle was designed by aviation engineer Joe Dudek, who based its shape on that of the 4,000mph X-15 experimental aircraft he had worked on. The single unsupercharged Bonneville engine was prepared at Johnson

Motors. Bored out to nearly 670cc and run for the records with nitro-methane in the fuel, it had cams ground by Californian tuning wizard Tim Witham, who worked closely with Triumph. He and Art Sparkes joined forces to form S&W, which made components such as high-performance valve springs marketed by Triumph Corp in the US and fitted to racing engines in Meriden's experimental department.

Having steadily developed and honed the Bonneville for four seasons, Triumph would make fundamental changes to its flagship for 1963.

A rigid elbow guide prevents the throttle cable from drooping. An adjuster on the cable is useful for setting free play at the twistgrip.

This was the final year for the pre-unit construction 650cc engine, evolved from the original 1938 Speed Twin.

The side panel is released by turning the slotted retainer with a coin, to gain access to the tool kit.

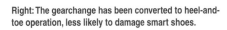

Right: The gearchange has been converted to heel-and-toe operation, less likely to damage smart shoes.

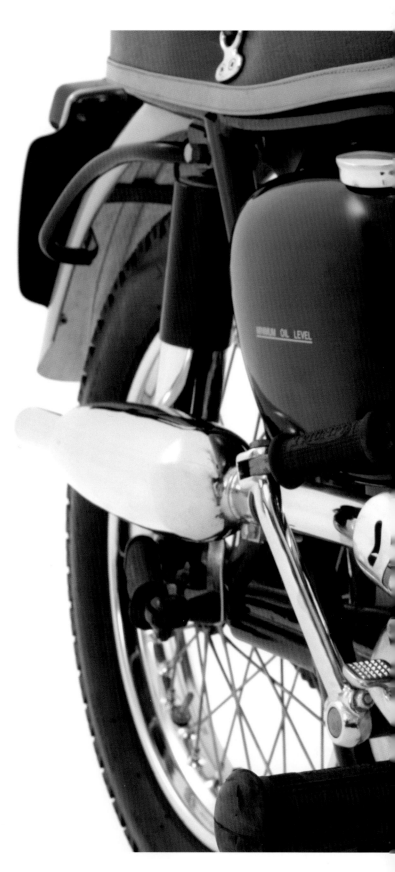

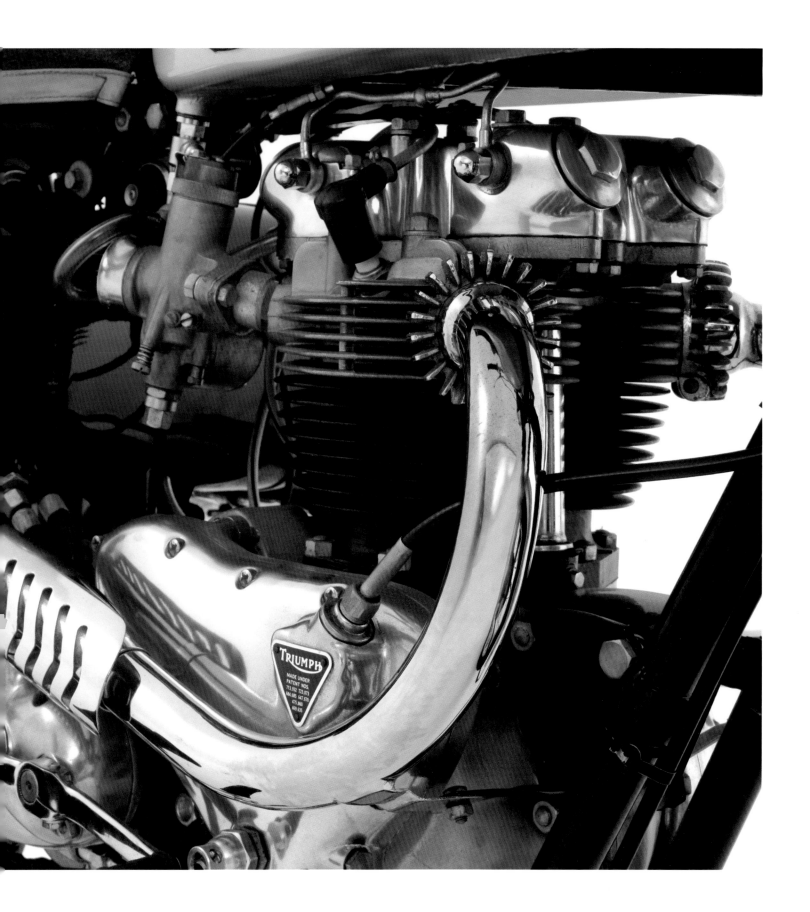

Black lettering on a gold ground was used on tank badges with the Flame and silver paint scheme.

The lighting switch is tucked under the front of the seat. A drilled frame lug immediately behind the centre stand is provided for sidecar attachment.

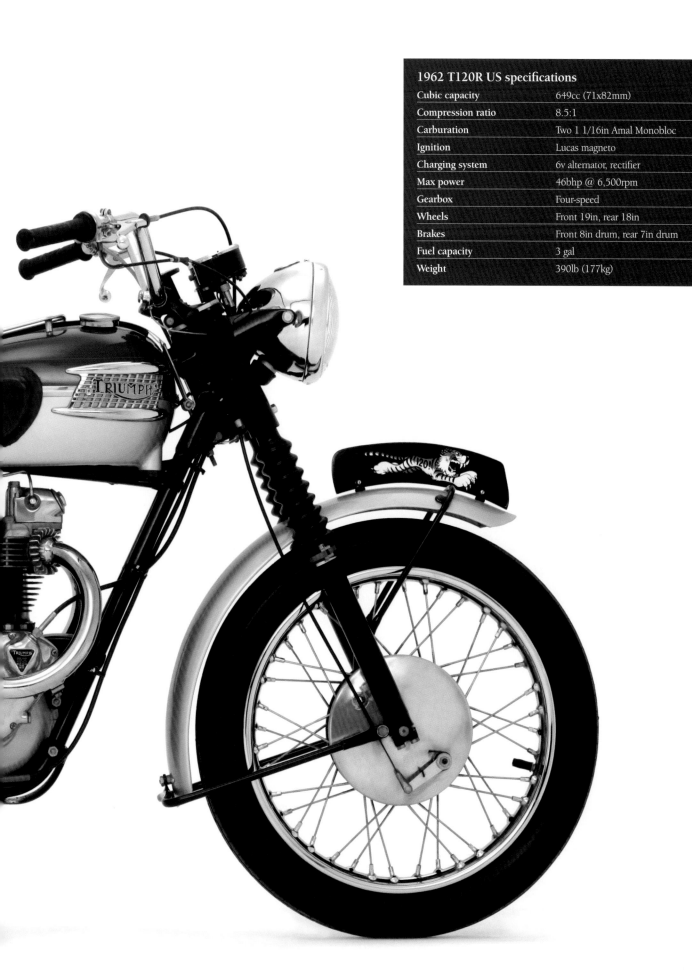

1962 T120R US specifications

Cubic capacity	649cc (71x82mm)
Compression ratio	8.5:1
Carburation	Two 1 1/16in Amal Monobloc
Ignition	Lucas magneto
Charging system	6v alternator, rectifier
Max power	46bhp @ 6,500rpm
Gearbox	Four-speed
Wheels	Front 19in, rear 18in
Brakes	Front 8in drum, rear 7in drum
Fuel capacity	3 gal
Weight	390lb (177kg)

1963 T120Rus

The Bonneville received a new look for year five, with major changes both to the mechanical and cycle parts. The engine and gearbox were now combined in one unit and a new frame reverted to single-downtube structure. There was no great performance increase, but the modernised machine carried the Bonneville legend forward at a time when opposition from rival products was growing.

Unit construction of the engine and transmission was applied to all 650cc Triumphs for 1963, following its debut on a 350cc twin in 1958 and subsequent application to 500cc models from the following year. The 150cc Terrier had been the first post-war unit machine but not Triumph's very first. That was the 350cc Model LS side-valve single with geared primary drive and an integral three-speed gearbox sold in 1926 and 1927.

Separate gearboxes were obsolete, harking back to the early days of multi-speed transmissions when factories, including Triumph, bought in proprietary 'boxes from specialist makers like Sturmey Archer.

Conceived by Edward Turner and overseen by chief engineer Bert Hopwood, formerly of BSA and Norton, the redesign enabled Triumph to pare down production costs and provided a response to the rival BSA company's latest flagship, the unit-construction A65

Star Twin launched a year earlier. Care was taken to preserve the familiar overall style of the power unit while giving it a sleeker, more streamlined form.

Not everyone approved of the unit-construction Bonnie: there were riders who missed the old Bonnie's rugged looks and believed the more rigid power unit made for a harsher ride.

Although little changed in appearance, the unit engine's top end was modified. Over time the previous cylinder head was prone to cracking between the valve seats and adjacent stud holes. The new design, soon to be known as the 'nine-stud head', featured an extra holding-down bolt near the centre and the other eight bolts' locations were dispersed. Obviously this necessitated changes to the cylinder barrel as well. The rocker boxes now had horizontal fins, harmonising with slightly extended head finning.

The notoriously errant inspection caps were now knurled round their outer circumference so that they could be retained by spring clips.

A new crankshaft, retaining the 85 per cent balance factor fixed on during 1962 production, had its timing-side nose modified to suit a garter seal now used to maintain oil pressure at the crank's end-feed point in the timing cover. The seal replaced an oft-neglected plain phosphor-bronze bush.

The magneto, which Lucas no longer wanted to supply, was replaced by coil ignition, standard on the 650cc Thunderbird tourer since 1954. The contact-breaker points were readily accessible, housed in the timing cover and driven by the exhaust camshaft. The other end of the camshaft was slotted to provide drive for a rev-counter, still listed as an extra.

The primary chain was upgraded to a duplex type. Tensioning, carried out by moving the gearbox relative to the engine on pre-unit machines, was now dealt with by an external adjuster at the base of the chaincase. A durable three-spring, six-plate clutch replaced the

Blending of the engine and gearbox into one unit was accomplished for 1963 without radically altering the Bonneville's looks.

71

four-spring type fitted to Triumph six-fifties since 1959.

A longer silencer known to the factory as the resonator type appeared on the T120 and T120R road models but not the T120C street scrambler variant.

Designed by draughtsman Brian Jones, who had followed Hopwood from Norton, the new frame had a stout 1 5/8in-diameter front downtube to which the two engine cradle tubes were brazed. While the rear subframe was still a separate bolted-up assembly, rigidity was enhanced by stronger support for the swinging arm, with the pivot now lent extra anchoring at each end by the rear engine plates. In 1962 yet more talent arrived from Norton, whose factory was being moved from Birmingham to London. The thoughtful and painstaking Doug Hele was to play a leading role in onward development of the Bonneville, both in improving performance and transforming its roadholding.

The front fork was unchanged from the previous 1962 chassis, but would be revised with external springs and improved damping by 1964.

The seat was little changed in form and still had a pale grey top panel, but it was now a hinge-up type giving easy access to the toolkit and electrical system's single 35-amp fuse underneath.

For the first time on a Bonneville the fuel tank was a single colour, a distinctive Alaskan White, also applied to the mudguards with gold central stripes.

This 1963 T120R from the Ace Classics collection is an American export, equipped with a rev-counter.

Handlebars of conventional 7/8in diameter were adopted from 1963 and their fixing clamps bedded in rubber anti-vibration bushes. The 1962 type of front fork was retained for a further year.

UK registrations gained a letter suffix to denote the year from 1963. Triumph would provide a suitably deeper plate in 1964. This re-import from the US has an age-related number fixed on the original plate.

MINIMUM OIL LEVEL

Steel plates securing the rear of the power unit to the frame also support the ends of the long swinging-arm pivot. Handling is improved as a result.

The coil ignition system's contact-breaker points are under a chromed inspection cap on the timing cover.

A twin-pull twistgrip is adopted in 1963,
as is the single air filter unit serving both
carburettors for US exports only. The rider's
footrests are looped under the exhaust pipes.

A new, longer silencer known at the factory
as the Resonator was fitted from 1963.

1963 T120R US specifications

Cubic capacity	649cc (71x82mm)
Compression ratio	8.5:1
Carburation	Two 1 1/16in Amal 376 Monobloc
Ignition	Lucas magneto
Max power	47bhp @ 6,700rpm
Gearbox	Four-speed
Wheels	Front 19in, rear 18in
Brakes	Front 8in drum, rear 7in drum
Fuel capacity	4 gal
Weight	365lb (166kg)

1965
T120
THRUXTON

Of all the Meriden Bonnevilles, the Thruxton may not be the most beautiful, but it wins on charisma. There are two reasons for that: markedly sharper performance than the stock T120, and great rarity. Fewer than 40 genuine examples of the Bonneville Thruxton are known to exist.

From 1955, a long-distance race strictly for production machines was staged annually at the Thruxton circuit in Hampshire. Originally of nine hours duration, it was fixed at a 500-mile distance (about 220 laps of the 2.4-mile circuit) in 1958. Although factory entries were barred, major manufacturers were keen to gain publicity by winning the '500 Miler'. So it wasn't surprising that favoured dealers entered ostensibly standard machines, cunningly tweaked at the factory while staying more or less within the rules.

Triumph took this a step further by selling a race-modified T120, so it could qualify for Production events. Launched at the 1964 Earls Court Show, the Bonneville Thruxton cost about 10 per cent

Modifications for track riding make the limited-edition Thruxton look quite different from the standard models.

more than a stock T120.

Forty-nine Bonnevilles were converted to Thruxton spec by Meriden fitters on overtime in May 1965. Allegedly, there should have been 50, but it was found that one cylinder head and its carburettors had disappeared. They were sent to selected dealers who often earmarked them for promising racers rather than selling to customers off the street.

The specification of the new model was drawn up by experimental department chief Doug Hele. Prior to joining Triumph he had been behind

Norton's Thruxton wins in 1960 and 1962 and saw racing as a useful development tool.

This Thruxton, owned by Geoff Parker, was originally despatched to the Lawton & Wilson dealership in Southampton. Co-proprietor Syd Lawton had won at Thruxton with Nortons, but switched to Triumph for 1965. In that year, the poor state of the Thruxton track saw the 500 Miler switched to the Castle Combe circuit in Wiltshire and this machine was ridden to victory by London motorcycle shop owner Dave Degens and Lawton's son Barry.

The Avonaire fairing, manufactured for Triumph by Mitchenall Bros, was an option that theoretically boosted speed, although the advantage over a 'naked' machine on a short, twisty circuit like Castle Combe would be minimal.

Turned-down handlebars, rear-set footrests and a single seat with a rest at the rear helped a racing crouch to be maintained. Although seen on the show model and this example, a tank-top parcel grid was not usually fitted, but could usefully hold a sponge pad for the rider to lean on. The rear frame

loop has lugs for attaching racing number plates.

Key chassis changes improved handling. Following factory tester Percy Tait's trials with different steering-head angles, the rake was reduced from 65 to 62 degrees. Front-fork damping was improved by shuttle valves and rear-wheel rim size increased to 19in, for better cornering clearance. An air scoop and outlet vent on the front brake reduced 'brake fade' caused by overheating.

The cigar-shaped silencers, clearly different from the standard Bonneville items, are part of an

Known at Triumph as 'M bars' the handlebars help the rider tuck down behind the fairing's screen.

Suitable for road or racing, the Avonaire fairing accepts the standard headlamp. Extra ventilation is provided for the front brake, which would have racing grade linings for track use. Up-tilted silencers are as seen on 1966 factory racers.

Smiths magnetic instruments replaced the
chronometric type from 1964. For racing, the
speedometer was sometimes taped over to
avoid distraction.

exhaust system Hele devised to gain maximum performance while keeping noise at an acceptable level for Production racing or road use. The header pipes are bridged by a balancer tube, so that each cylinder exhausts into both silencers. Just below the cross-tube, the 1 1/2in main pipes narrow to 1 1/4in, promoting higher gas speed. Tilted to optimise cornering clearance, the silencers are supported by steel

hangers fixed to the rear frame loop.

As happens with racing machines, this one was updated with later fork yokes and Amal Concentric carburettors. Originally, the 1965 Thruxton had 1 1/8in Amal Monoblocs and Amal's 510 'matchbox' remote float bowl, flexibly mounted. To further avoid frothing due to vibration, the carburettors mount on short lengths of flexible hose. Triumph

made a special oil tank with a cutaway to clear the right-side intake trumpet.

Inside the engine, valve gear modifications permit higher rpm and raise power output to 48bhp. Hele increased valve lift, prolonged openings and reduced cam-lobe wear by using cam followers with wide-radius feet. For the first time on a catalogued T120, a positive oil supply fed the exhaust cams,

which benefited less than their inlet counterparts from lubricant flung off the crankshaft. Close-ratio four-speed gearbox clusters were available to order.

A few more Production racing T120s were prepared for dealers after the main 1965 batch went out and full-works Bonneville Production racers fielded successfully from 1966 to 1969 are often referred to as Thruxtons.

Weight is saved by using tank transfers instead of the roadsters' badges. Decorative fairing stickers have been added by an owner.

The front hub has no chrome cover and is perforated to improve cooling by ventilation and usefully reduce unsprung weight.

Above: Amal Concentric carburettors, available from 1967, have been fitted here. Originally this 1965 machine would have been equipped with the earlier Monoblocs and a remote float.

Right: Footrests are moved back onto the rear engine plates and the gearchange lever reversed.

1965 T120 Thruxton specifications

Cubic capacity	649cc (71x82mm)
Compression ratio	11:1
Carburation	Two Amal 30mm Concentric
Ignition	Lucas magneto
Charging system	6v alternator
Max power	50bhp @ 6,500rpm
Gearbox	Four-speed
Wheels	Front 19in, rear 18in
Brakes	Front 8in drum, rear 7in drum
Fuel capacity	4 gal
Weight	390lb (177kg)

Long cigar-shaped silencers exclusive to the Thruxton
are tilted up to gain cornering clearance.

Aerodynamic benefits of a fairing come into their own on longer race circuits. The Dunlop K81 TT100 tyres fitted became available from 1970.

UK registrations with suffix letters for year forced makers to fit deeper number plates. Stays fixed to the rear subframe support the weight of the silencers.

1965
T120C
COMPETITION SPORTS

High-level exhaust pipes identify this handsome tool as a T120C, the Competition variant of the Bonneville designed specifically for American sport riders.

Weekend competition riding was booming in Sixties America. The wide-open spaces of the western states were ideal for cross-country scrambles or Hare and Hounds races, often run on a point-to-point basis rather than on a short circuit in the European way. Elsewhere, riders pitted themselves against the natural landscape in events like the gruelling Jack Pine Enduro in the wooded and watery terrain of the mid-western state of Michigan or the Alligator Enduro in the near-jungle of swampy central Florida.

A more spectator-oriented sport was TT Scrambles or TT Steeplechase. Said to have been originally inspired by photographs of machines airborne in the Isle of Man TT road races, American-style TT was a spectacular form of dirt-track racing, with an artificial motocross-style jump, usually staged on artificial circuits but sometimes on a natural course like that of the legendary Peoria TT.

This Bonneville T120C road-legal street scrambler is as supplied through Triumph's eastern

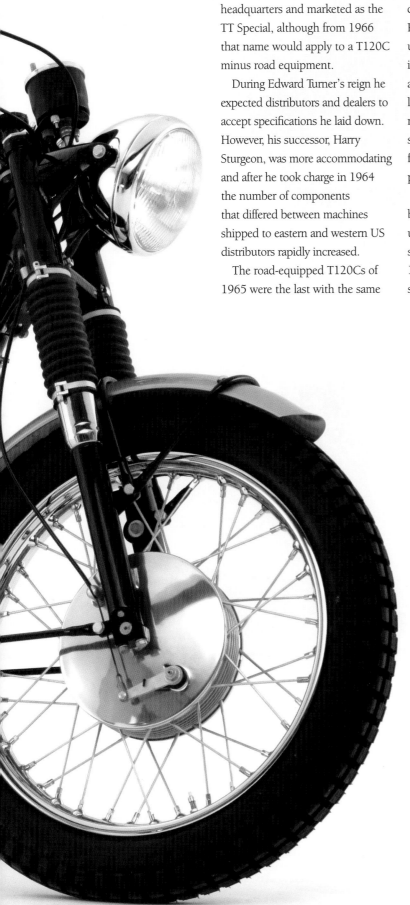

headquarters and marketed as the TT Special, although from 1966 that name would apply to a T120C minus road equipment.

During Edward Turner's reign he expected distributors and dealers to accept specifications he laid down. However, his successor, Harry Sturgeon, was more accommodating and after he took charge in 1964 the number of components that differed between machines shipped to eastern and western US distributors rapidly increased.

The road-equipped T120Cs of 1965 were the last with the same

colours used for all Bonnevilles: Pacific Blue and silver. The upswept exhausts, which terminate in short silencers, have heat shields attached where the rider's legs are likely to make contact. Unlike most road Bonnevilles of the period, the seat is plain black, more practical for off-roading than the pale top panel on two-tone covers.

Both Monobloc carburettors breathe through a single air filter unit containing a paper element, seen on export machines from 1963 to 1965. Like many British sports machines, early Bonnevilles

had unfiltered carburettors that let the last ounce of power be used but did nothing to prevent bore wear due to the ingress of grit and dust. Even when filters were introduced, overseas dealers were concerned about their effectiveness. Meriden service manager John Nelson recalls an Australian making his point by bringing to the factory a box full of dust that he had emptied out of filters.

On the left side, the filter housing made the lighting and ignition switches even harder to access. They had been

The T120C for the eastern US follows a dual-purpose road/off-road pattern set by Triumph's single carburettor TR6 Trophy. No passenger footrests are provided.

This machine's Smiths speedometer
has been replaced by a compact VDO
item marketed by Tri-Cor.

inconveniently placed on the side panel since 1963.

Triumph engineers were concerned about main bearing and primary drive problems resulting from the greater rigidity of the unit-construction crankcase castings. During 1964 production a major revision was tried. Location of the crankshaft was no longer fixed at the timing-side main bearing but on the opposite side, where the engine sprocket boss now tightened up against the inner bearing race.

Engine timing was made easier by a removable threaded plug located behind the cylinder barrel on the right-hand crankcase half. A tool holding a sliding rod was inserted. When the rod dropped into a recess on the crankshaft flywheel, the engine was accurately pegged at top-dead-centre.

An improved front fork, with stronger bellows-type gaiters, had been specified since 1964, as had rider's footrests now fixed to the rear engine plates instead of the lower frame tubes. The oddly shaped rear stop and tail lamp seen here only appeared on 1965-season export machines. No longer concealed under the seat, the Lucas horn hung from the frame on a bracket below the fuel tank – not a pretty sight but it could at least be heard better.

Competition models crossed the Atlantic shod with Dunlop's Trials Universal Tyres, suitable for general but not extreme off-road use. Owners could subsequently opt for treads more appropriate to the type of riding they did.

Triumph switched from Smiths Chronometric speedometers and rev-counters to magnetic instruments with more modern face graphics in 1964, but this machine sports a German-made VDO speedometer. Carrying the Tri-Cor logo on its face, it was one of many aftermarket accessories marketed by Triumph's eastern US headquarters.

This rare and painstakingly restored machine is from the stable of Graham Bowen, who tracked it down at a vintage motorcycle swapmeet in the Chicago area. Britain's foremost private restorer of Triumph twins, Graham goes to great lengths to find the correct parts – such as spark plugs, control cables and tyres – that make the difference between an average restoration and an outstanding one.

1965 would be the last year for Triumph's iconic chromed grille badges, used since 1957.

Above: The ignition key can be seen in its switch, awkwardly located between the air filter and the side panel.

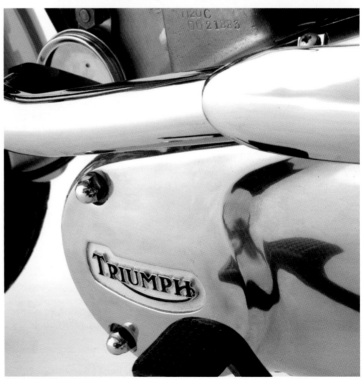

Right: Heat shields are fitted over the high-level exhaust pipes.

Far right: A steel plate protects the lower engine from damage when rough-riding. No longer hidden, the horn is now more audible.

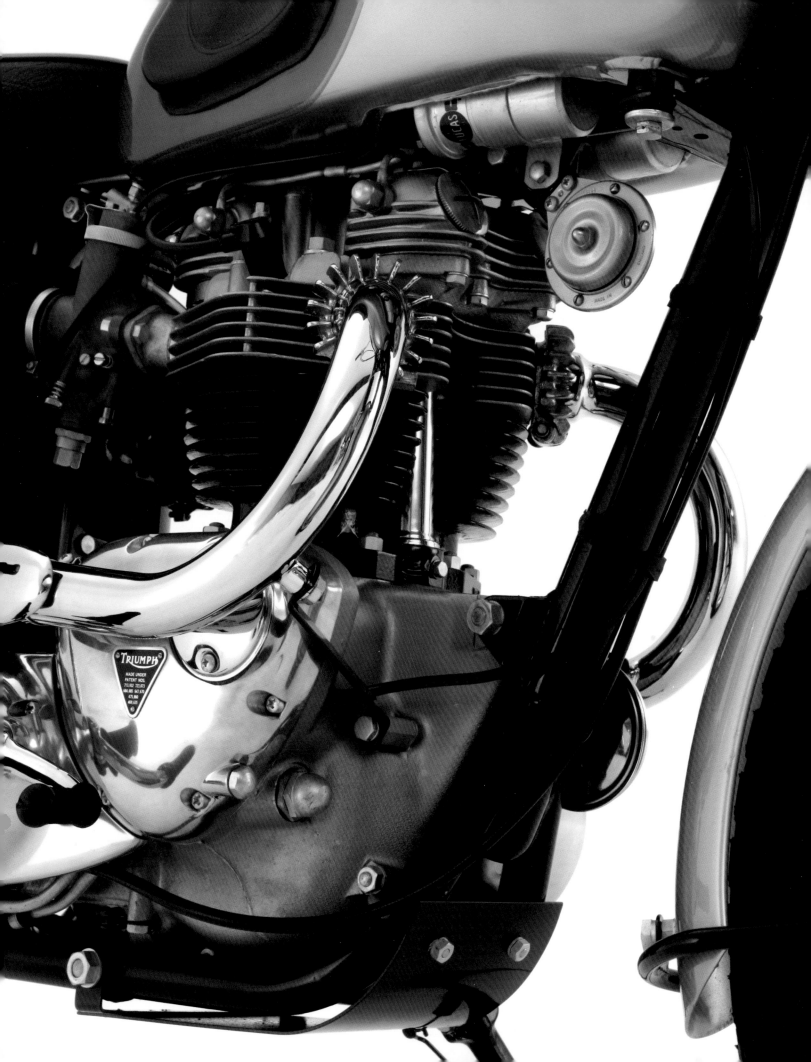

1965 T120C Competition Sports specifications	
Cubic capacity	649cc (71x82mm)
Compression ratio	8.5:1
Carburation	Two 1 1/16in Amal Monobloc
Ignition	Lucas magneto
Max power	46bhp
Gearbox	Four-speed
Wheels	Front 19in, rear 18in
Brakes	Front 8in drum, rear 7in drum
Fuel capacity	3 gal
Weight	385lb (175kg)

This handsome eastern US variant of the Bonneville was only made for three seasons and the 1965 type is particularly rare.

1966 T120 UK

With its Grenadier Red and white colour scheme, the 1966 Bonneville stood out proudly in any line of motorcycles parked at a café, bar or race meeting. The bright new model reflected Triumph's confidence as a marque at the top of its game. In a survey of owners carried out by *Motor Cycle* magazine in 1965, 99 per cent said that their Bonneville was a good buy and overall marks given

for acceleration were 100/100. Sales were booming, not just in the UK and the fast-growing North American markets but right across the globe. The Bonneville defined the dynamism and style of the British sporting motorcycle.

Changing a popular logo is always risky, but Triumph boldly adopted a new tank emblem for 1966 models. While the familiar lettering was retained, the 'harmonica' grille gave way

to a plainer device, sometimes called the 'eyebrow' badge. A less popular move was a change to pale grey handlebar grips. Rider's gloves, and especially waxed cotton waterproof over-mitts, soon made them look grubby. A return to black grips was made during 1966 production.

Numerous technical improvements were incorporated for the new season. One of the most important was the revised frame, a spin-off from Triumph's Production racing exploits overseen by chief development engineer Doug Hele. The steering-head angle was altered from

The new style of tank badge and grey handlebar grips are clearly visible, while the frame's altered steering head angle is not so obvious.

65 degrees to 62 degrees, a change previously made on the 1965 Thruxton specials, to improve high-speed stability. The new frame incorporated lugs on the front of the steering stem for mounting a fairing as used by police fleets and owners fitting aftermarket equipment. Better stopping power was provided by a new design of front hub with wider brake shoes impacting on a greater drum surface.

To boost engine performance the compression ratio was slightly raised from 8.5:1 to 9:1 and hotter cams were installed with followers developed for racing engines and a pressurised oil supply fed to the exhaust cams. Crankshaft rotation tended to splash ambient oil on to the inlet lobes but not the exhaust cams, which usually wore much faster. To gain a livelier throttle response, the crankshaft's flywheel ring was made roughly 2 1/2lb (1kg) lighter. For the first time in a T120 engine, there was now a roller main bearing on the drive side and crankshaft location reverted to being fixed at the timing side.

Uprating the electrical system to 12 volts was a significant modernisation. Having traditionally viewed six volts as sufficient for motorcycles without electric starting, Triumph persuaded Lucas

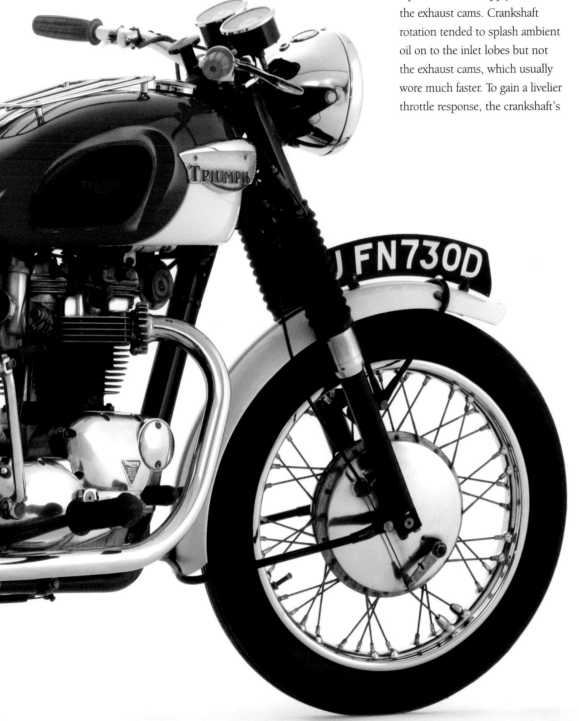

to provide 12-volt equipment for 1966 Bonnevilles, although pairs of six-volt batteries linked in series were fitted in early production. The alternator's AC current was converted to DC by a multi-plate rectifier as before, but a Zener diode was now used to regulate battery charging. It converted surplus current into heat and dispersed it through the aluminium plate it was mounted on. A prominent engine cut-out on the right handlebar was easily reached by the rider's thumb.

A rev-counter was now a standard item and the routing of its drive cable was much improved by adding a gear unit at the camshaft take-off, to turn the drive through 90 degrees.

During 1966, Triumph's reputation for speed was further enhanced by a new Bonneville record that bettered Bill Johnson's 230mph run of 1962. Bob Leppan, proprietor of Triumph Detroit, raised the absolute world record to 245.667mph. The laboriously prepared and tested Gyronaut streamliner he piloted across the Salt Flats was powered by two unsupercharged pre-unit 650cc engines running on alcohol fuel. Triumph boasted of the achievement with a decal proclaiming 'World's Fastest Motorcycle' for the next four years.

But difficulties loomed in the US. Edward Turner, 'Father of the Triumph Twin', had retired in 1964. Harry Sturgeon came from BSA-owned Churchill machine tools company to take charge of BSA and Triumph motorcycle business. A dynamic and demanding boss, he did much to chase American sales. However, he upset Triumph staff by merging the two makes' US operations during 1966, despite the intense rivalry – even enmity – that existed between them. Struck by a brain tumour, Sturgeon died in 1967 and was replaced by the unsuitable Lionel Jofeh. Another problem was the ever-growing Japanese motorcycle industry, which was shipping nearly half a million two-wheelers to the US annually, against less than 35,000 from Britain.

This UK machine has covered less than 15,000 miles since 1966 and is still shod with its original tyres. After only a couple of years on the road it was stored in the owner's front room and is now owned by Ace Classics.

Above: The uprated front brake's hub has a spoke flange of a larger diameter than the brake backplate, seen on 1966 and 1967 machines only.

Right: A large cut-out button is mounted on the right handlebar.

Drive for the rev-counter, taken off the inlet
camshaft on the left side of the crankcase, is
now by a tidy right-angle unit. Discoloured fuel
lines testify that this is an unrestored machine.

Above: A longer lever aids kick-starting with the slightly higher compression specified for 1966.

Far left: The lighting switch and ignition switch are both mounted in the left side panel on T120s from 1963 to 1966.

Left: The stop light switch, triggered by the movement of the brake operating rod, is vulnerable to road dirt and corrosion.

1966 T120 UK specifications

Cubic capacity	649cc (71x82mm)
Compression ratio	9:1
Carburation	Two Amal 1 1/8in Monobloc
Ignition	Battery and coil
Charging system	12v alternator
Max power	47bhp @ 6,700rpm
Gearbox	Four-speed
Wheels	Front 19in, rear 18in
Brakes	Front 8in, rear 7in
Fuel capacity	4 gal
Weight	365lb (166kg)

With raised compression, stronger valve springs and a lighter flywheel, the 1966 T120 is a strong performer. Few survive in standard trim, possibly because they were converted into café racers or ridden into the ground.

1966
T120C
TT SPECIAL

No Bonneville looks meaner or sleeker than the T120C TT Special and the 1966 version is arguably the most attractive of the US Competition variants. Like the road T120R Bonneville sold on the US market in that year, it is finished in Alaskan White with Grenadier Red stripes running over the top of its slimmed 2.5 US gallon (2 Imperial gallon) fuel tank. A broad central band is flanked by two narrower stripes, all edged with gold pin-striping. The seat is a functional all-black one, as seen on the majority of C variants.

This restored eastern US example

has white mudguards with single central red stripes. Whether many TTs actually had painted guards is a matter of contention among restorers. Stainless steel guards, as fitted to the T120R, made more sense for serious rough riding. Western TTs had light alloy guards.

Unlike the T120C street scrambler, the T120C TT (coded T120TT from partway through 1966 production) is a pure competition machine without road equipment such as silencers, lights, speedometer and horn. A loud and exhilarating ride, the TT was in the Triumph range from 1963 to 1967, produced in much smaller numbers than the road Bonnevilles.

TT is a specific form of American dirt racing in which the 500cc capacity limit applied to overhead-valve engines in flat track racing until 1969 did not apply. Triumph was prominent in the sport in the Sixties, when two spectacular West Coast-based TT stars rode the marque to countless successes.

They were Skip Van Leeuwen, known as 'Van Loony', and the exuberant Eddie Mulder, who would be Clint Eastwood's stunt double in the 1973 movie *Magnum Force*. When the first 1965 TT Special landed at Johnson Motors,

US models for 1966 have the same paint colours as home market machines but with a strikingly different scheme for the smaller fuel tank.

Mulder won a TT on it at Ascot Park in Gardenia, California, virtually out of the crate. No one was a greater fan of the TT than Mulder. Still active in vintage competition, he rides, builds and sells the Eddie Mulder replica, based on the original TT Special. 'It was the cat's miaow,' he says.

Clearly ready-made for the job, which involved riding through left and right turns and over high jumps, the fiery TT was also ideal for a variety of other competitive events including scrambles and even drag racing.

Early TTs had upswept exhausts, but from 1965 large-diameter (1.75in) tubes were used, converging to run close together under the power unit and ending short of the rear wheel. A distinctive hallmark feature, they are supported by the frame lugs normally used as centre-stand pivots on road Bonnevilles. Needless to say, the sound they emit is awesome although it was not unknown for TT Specials to be ridden on the highway in less heavily regulated states. Triumph listed exhaust flutes, small devices that could be inserted in plain exhaust pipes to take the worst out of their bark.

High-compression 11:1 pistons pep up engine output, as does a special cylinder head to which Amal Monobloc carburettors with 1 3/16in bores are fitted in place of

With its uncluttered looks, the pure competition Bonneville also sounds good, thanks to those open exhaust pipes.

The TT Special engine contains high-compression pistons and alternator-powered Energy Transfer ignition.

the road models' 1 1/8in size.

The US monthly *Cycle World* reported several 120mph-plus straight-line runs with an early T120C TT. When Meriden's experimental department built a small batch of Production-class road racers to be ridden by factory riders in 1967, they started out with TTs taken from the assembly line.

To save weight and avoid acid spills in the rough and tumble of off-roading, Triumph specified a battery-less Energy Transfer AC ignition system supplied by Lucas for its pure competition machines. It is powered directly from an ET alternator and the ignition coils are activated by contact breakers in the usual way.

Dirt-track racers don't need a parcel rack and none is seen here, but the tank-top item was attached to earlier TTs. John Nelson, service chief at Meriden through the Sixties, has explained that when production was running at full-tilt it could be more cost-effective to fit such components across the board than have to deal with numerous trim variations.

However, Triumph stopped fitting racks to US-export road machines in 1967 because of an American customer who claimed to have been castrated by the grid in an accident and took protracted legal actions against Triumph. From 1969, UK and general export Bonnevilles no longer had the rack, which owners had found useful for carrying over-trousers or a map case.

Graham Bowen was given this machine as the bare essentials of engine cases and frame by a friend in the American Midwest. He brought it to the UK for restoration as airline baggage.

Separate air filters for each carburettor, with perforated chromed cases, appeared during 1966 production.

Ready for the dirt track or desert scramble,
the TT is lithe and functional.

No speedometer is fitted. The ignition cut-out is placed close to the throttle twistgrip.

Tucked in to aid cornering clearance, the elegant TT pipes usefully blow detritus off the rear tyre.

1966 T120C TT Special specifications

Cubic capacity	649cc (71x82mm)
Compression ratio	11:1
Carburation	Two 1 1/16in Amal Monobloc
Ignition	Energy Transfer with coils
Charging system	Not fitted
Max power	52bhp
Gearbox	Four-speed
Wheels	Front 19in, rear 18in
Brakes	Front 8in drum, rear 7in drum
Fuel capacity	2 gal
Weight	350lb (159kg)

TT Specials left the factory fitted with Dunlop
Trials Universal tyres, the front cover being
wider than on road machines.

1968 T120
UK & GENERAL EXPORT

The Bonneville, and Triumph motorcycles generally, were riding high when the latest edition of the T120 was announced late in 1967. A few months earlier the Bonnie's prowess had been proved in a new race for street bikes held on the long and difficult Isle of Man TT circuit.

The 750cc class of the inaugural Production TT was won by seasoned international racer John Hartle on a factory-prepared Bonneville, averaging 97mph over three laps of the 37.73-mile Mountain Course. Victory was particularly sweet for Triumph as rival 750cc Norton Atlas and 650cc BSA Spitfire entries had to settle for second and third places respectively. In addition, Bonnevilles were first and second in a Production marathon held on the Brands Hatch circuit that year.

Marque prestige in America was reinforced when factory rider Gary Nixon took Triumph's first Grand National championship. Most of his successes were on 500cc machines in a series where riders earned points on both dirt and asphalt tracks. But when speed-hungry stateside riders went out to buy a Triumph, they were likely to plump for the Bonneville flagship.

This is the UK and general export machine for 1968, with Hi-fi Scarlet and silver paint. Another conspicuous change for the year, appreciated by hard riders, was a front brake with twin-leading-shoe operation. The drum was still of 8in diameter, but each shoe was now activated by its

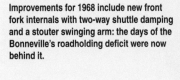

Improvements for 1968 include new front fork internals with two-way shuttle damping and a stouter swinging arm: the days of the Bonneville's roadholding deficit were now behind it.

own cam so that the leading edges of both were pressed against the drum, creating a self-servo effect for sharper retardation. Specified on both Triumph and BSA models, the 'twin-leader' had a horizontal stop for the outer cable low down on the backplate and the inner pulled on the cam levers, connected by a linkage. The long cable made for poor feel and tended to snag, so

a revision was made for 1969: the stop was moved to the upper part of the plate and a bell-crank lever used for the front cam.

Also clearly visible is the new type of Zener diode heat sink below the headlamp. The finned aluminium casting's front-facing position on the lower fork yoke exposes it to cooling air on the move.

Roadholding, no longer a weak

point on the 650cc twins, was further enhanced by the adoption of shuttle valves to provide consistent damping in the front fork. This was one of the tweaks originally developed in Doug Hele's experimental department for racing and carried over to production.

Amal's latest Concentric carburettor had been introduced

during the previous year's production. Its float bowl surrounds the jet block, rather than being set to one side as on the Monobloc. The format, previously used by the Villiers two-stroke engine company, helped Amal make an instrument at the low price expected by the BSA group. Air filters, already fitted to export machines, became standard on home-market T120s during production for 1968 and their casings were now threaded on to the carburettor intakes.

Upgrades inside the engine included positive oil supply for the wear-prone exhaust camshaft, revised oiling arrangements for the valve-operating rockers, stronger valve springs, and pistons with more metal in their crowns.

The monthly *Motorcycle Mechanics* reported hitting a top speed of 115mph in speed tests of a 1968 Bonneville conducted as part of a 1,000-mile test. The only fault encountered was with build quality: by the time the machine had been ridden from Meriden to London, a headlamp bolt had vibrated loose and dropped off.

Such problems, and a few worse ones, were probably inevitable with a factory that had gone from producing around 250 machines a week at the start of the Sixties to as many as 1,200 units by this time. Large numbers of shop-floor staff had to be recruited, many of them coming from other automotive plants in the Coventry area, so the cosy old days when virtually everyone in the building was a dedicated motorcycle enthusiast were gone. Pay rates were excellent and several trades unions were strongly represented, from the giant Transport & General Workers Union to smaller unions for metalworkers and clerical staff.

Disputes and stoppages were not uncommon, but long-suffering works manager John Walford used both firmness and flexibility to keep the lines going. The Triumph Engineering arm of the BSA group never made a loss.

This fine example of a 1968 Bonneville in UK and general export trim has been owned by Hugh Brown since being acquired as a non-runner in 1977. During a more recent rebuild he dynamically balanced the crankshaft. Smooth running is a quality he claims as a speciality at his Hertfordshire restoration business The Bike Shed.

A steering damper was no longer considered necessary, although it could still be requested as an option. Bonneville transfer in script appeared on the tank top for 1968.

The front hub's plated left-side cover now has ten slots around its circumference.

Above left: A World Record transfer was worn on the left fork shroud for four seasons, following the 1965 245.6mph Bonneville record.

Above: Braking is greatly improved by a front drum with twin leading shoe operation, for maximum self-servo effect. This cable arrangement only lasted one year.

Left: This was the third and final year for the 'eyebrow' style of fuel tank badge.

During 1967 production Amal's latest 930 Concentric carburettor replaced the Monobloc type used since 1959. Float tickler extensions available later have been fitted.

An inspection cover with three screws is now provided on the primary chaincase for access to the timing marks on the alternator rotor.

1968 T120 UK & General Export specifications	
Cubic capacity	649cc (71x82mm)
Compression ratio	9:1
Carburation	Two Amal 30mm Concentric
Ignition	Battery and coil
Charging system	12v alternator, Zener diode
Max power	47bhp @ 6,700rpm
Gearbox	Four-speed
Wheels	Front 19in, rear 18in
Brakes	Front 8in sls drum, rear 7in sls drum
Fuel capacity	4 gal
Weight	365lb (166kg)

The definitive Sixties' roadburner. This version of the
650cc Bonneville is one of the most sought-after today.

1968 T120R US

While the American-market T120R for 1968 shares the Hi-fi Scarlet and silver paint scheme of the UK and general export version, the arrangement of its colours on the slimmer US fuel tank is quite different, with the red predominant. The mudguards (or fenders, in US parlance) are unpainted stainless steel, as seen on export T120s since 1966.

The transatlantic edition is also identified by side reflectors, added to improve night-time visibility.

They became mandatory under new construction regulations introduced in the wake of US campaigner Ralph Nader's drive to make America's vehicles and highways safer. Red reflector panels flank the polished aluminium rear lamp bracket and orange discs mount under the front of the fuel tank, making removal of the tank a more fiddly job.

Several new '68 features for all markets made maintenance easier. Twin Lucas 6CA ignition contact breaker points were a boon in

Higher 'bars, smaller fuel tank and shorter silencer are among the features distinguishing the US variant for 1968.

offering independent setting for each cylinder, while a detachable cover on the primary chaincase made timing the spark with a strobe light a simpler job. On later 1968 engines a static timing marker was added adjacent to the marked alternator rotor, so timing could be set by eye if necessary. More precise ignition timing meant smoother running and happier customers.

During 1968 production the cylinder base flange nuts, plain hexagons since Bonneville production started, were changed to a 12-point pattern. They would now all accept an appropriate ring spanner, overcoming an accessibility problem previously cursed by service staff and home mechanics.

Other detail improvements had made the Bonneville more rider-friendly. They included moving the ignition switch from its side-panel location to a more accessible site on the left-side headlamp bracket, while a longer, curved side stand lessened the risk of toppling. Since 1967 the seat's grey top panel had been quilted into bars running across its width and the rear portion was slightly raised to help passenger security, while the

western US edition's grab strap was discontinued. Instead a rear grab rail was introduced during 1968 production, although it does not feature on the machine seen here. For hard riders, handling had to be marginally enhanced by a beefed-up swinging arm for the rear suspension and the thicker-walled front downtube introduced during production. While the specified

front tyre section for home-market models was slimmed from 3.25 to 3.00 in 1967 with a ribbed tread, US machines kept the wider size.

The Smiths magnetic speedometer was now calibrated to 150mph – surely a source of satisfaction for many Bonneville owners even if 115mph was a more realistic maximum for a machine in top condition.

In the late Sixties, Triumph was one of Britain's most important dollar earners and the BSA group, which sold motorcycles in 150 countries, won the Queen's Award for Industry in 1966 and 1967. But change was in the air. In 1968 BSA and Triumph

engineers were preoccupied with the autumn launch of the first model to displace the Bonneville at the top of Triumph's range: the 750cc three-cylinder BSA Rocket 3 and Triumph Trident. An overhead-camshaft version of the 650cc twin had been prototyped with input from Edward Turner in his retirement, but it was junked because of overheating problems and a disappointing power gain.

After the untimely death of BSA group managing director Harry Sturgeon, another non-motorcyclist, Lionel Jofeh, took charge of BSA and Triumph. Arriving from the aviation industry, he wanted to modernise and

rationalise the whole operation. While astute, he was a poor communicator and calamitously unreceptive to advice from old hands. He set up a joint research and development centre for both marques at Umberslade Hall, a grand edifice in rural Warwickshire, installing new design and engineering talent. Some of those recruited had no motorcycling experience and when little of much practical use emerged, the facility became jokingly known among factory staff as Slumberglade Hall. Doug Hele and his experimental department staff resolutely refused to move to the house in the country.

One of the future projects being undertaken there was the redesign of both BSA and Triumph six-fifties, coded P39. Dr Stefan Bauer, a nuclear physicist who had previously contributed to Norton Commando development, had the job of designing a frame for the new models, using computer technology to analyse stresses in a tubular structure. When eventually introduced for the 1971 season, the new frame would cause havoc in production – and this marked a turning point in Meriden's fortunes.

The 1968 US-market T120R on these pages is another superb restoration by Essex-based 'concours king' Graham Bowen.

Distribution of the Hi-fi Scarlet and silver paint is markedly different from the UK version's scheme.

Above left: Stainless steel mudguards seen on US Triumphs from 1966 to 1970 are smart, strong and practical.

Above: The Zener diode and its finned heat-sink is now placed in the cooling air-stream.

Left: Lifting the hinged seat gives access to the oil filler cap and a 12-volt battery held by a flexible strap.

1968 T120R US specifications

Cubic capacity	649cc (71x82mm)
Compression ratio	9:1
Carburation	Two Amal 30mm Concentric
Ignition	Battery and coil
Charging system	12v alternator, Zener diode
Max power	47bhp @ 6,700rpm
Gearbox	Four-speed
Wheels	Front 19in, rear 18in
Brakes	Front 8in tls drum, rear 7in drum
Fuel capacity	2 gal
Weight	365lb (166kg)

Side reflectors, orange at the front and red at the rear, were added to conform to US highway regulations and improve night-time visibility.

1969 T120Rus

To the casual eye, one of the most obvious updates to the Bonneville for 1969 is a fresh look for the fuel tank. The cast zinc-alloy badge's shape is not radically altered but simplified. Less rounded and more angular, it followed industrial design trends of the time.

The paint colours were now silver, contrasted with a strong orangey-red listed as Olympic Flame (the XIX Olympiad had been held in 1968). A similar colour had been seen on the US-market T120R of seven years previously.

As can be seen on this US-market sixty-niner, the silver part was applied in a striking 'scalloped' form on transatlantic export versions. In adopting the scalloped style, Meriden's chief stylist, Jack Wickes, was following a vogue among Triumph customisers that had begun ten years before in the Motor City of Detroit. The look had become so popular that dealers sold new machines ready-painted with non-standard paint designs. Even before the 1969 range arrived, the style

had become synonymous with cool Triumphs. Later in production another silver 'claw' would be added below the tank badge.

The Girling rear suspension units also stand out, as the telescopic steel shrouds they had worn since 1959 are absent, exposing chrome-plated springs. These were not so easy to clean, but the bare look was coming into vogue for any machine

with sporting pretensions and fully enclosed springs looked staid.

Twin electric windtone horns supplied by Clear Hooters replace the previous single Lucas item. Not obtrusive, they are held on brackets on either side of the frame downtubes and have slightly domed plastic covers.

Not so obvious is the coupled exhaust system, with a cross-tube

Exposed springs on the rear suspension units and a cross-tube linking the exhaust downpipes are among new features for 1969. The twin-leading-shoe front brake first specified for 1968 has revised cable routing and lever arrangement.

like that seen on Production racing Bonnevilles since 1965. It serves a similar purpose, doubling the system's volume to minimise noise without hindering performance. Sound emissions were becoming an issue for motorcycle makers, although in the Sixties the US market wasn't difficult to satisfy in this regard, as it was to become in the Seventies. Some Triumph riders incorrectly assume that the balance pipe is detrimental to performance.

Meriden found plenty of detail improvements to make for the 20th season of its 650cc power unit. They included a cure for exhaust camshaft wear by case-hardening the shaft by a Nitriding process and a return to greater tractability by specifying a heavier crankshaft flywheel from early in 1968 production. Piston supplier Hepolite added further strengthening in the region of the crown and gudgeon pin, while detail changes to the pushrod tubes and their seals were made to combat oil weeps. Oil circulation was boosted by increasing the size of the pump's feed plunger and allowing more lubricant to build

The US variant has a passenger grab rail,
fixed to the seat base for this year only.

up in the crankcase sump before being scavenged. An oil pressure sensor fitted to the timing cover is wired to a warning light, added alongside the ammeter and full-beam light on the headlamp shell.

Triumph and BSA were in the costly process of moving over piecemeal from British Standard, Whitworth and Cycle thread forms to the Unified Thread Standard favoured by manufacturers in the US and Canada. For 1969, the 650cc crankcase halves and timing cover made the switch, along with

threads in the cylinder head.

The return to a heavier crankshaft flywheel and the greater tractability this produced – along with all the other refinements made to the T120 through the late Sixties – earned the 112mph 1969 and 1970 editions a reputation as the peak of Meriden 650cc Bonneville development, if not of build quality.

During 1969, Bonnevilles had a great year on race circuits. In the 750cc Production TT, factory rider Malcolm Uphill demolished

the lap record, breaking the 'ton' barrier with a circuit at 100.37mph and averaging 99.99mph for the three-lap, 114-mile race. The first 500-mile race for street bikes held at Thruxton since 1964 saw Bonnevilles dominate, taking the first three places ahead of a factory BSA twin, while the 750cc class of the midsummer Barcelona 24-hour marathon in Spain was won by Uphill with co-rider Steve Jolly. At Anderstorp in Sweden works Bonnevilles scooped the first four places in an international race.

Triumph rider Gene Romero was runner-up in America's glamorous multi-disciplinary Grand National series, where for the first time the 650cc Bonneville engine was eligible for flat track events.

The big news in the US in 1969 was the arrival of Honda's glittering new superbike – the CB750. With four cylinders, five speeds, electric starting, a disc front brake and cut-throat pricing, it was a daunting challenge to Britain's hold on the large-capacity, high-performance market.

Safety reflectors and twin Clear Hooter horns with domed plastic covers mount under the front of the fuel tank.

The steering damper, optional from 1968, is not fitted to this machine. A key slot for the steering lock is on the fork top yoke.

The front brake cable pulls on a bell-crank to rotate the operating cam spindles, which are linked by an adjustable rod.

The capital letters Bonneville transfer was first seen in 1969. Adding side reflectors necessitated a redesigned rear lamp unit.

1969 T120R US specifications

Cubic capacity	649cc (71x82mm)
Compression ratio	9:1
Carburation	Two Amal 30mm Concentric
Ignition	Battery and coil
Charging system	12v alternator, Zener diode
Max power	47bhp @ 6,500rpm
Gearbox	Four-speed
Wheels	Front 19in, rear 18in
Brakes	Front 8in tls drum, rear 7in drum
Fuel capacity	2 gal (2.5 US)
Weight	365lb (166kg)

The prop stand's curved leg was lengthened from 1968, to offer firmer support.

The tank badge change for 1969 is accompanied on US machines by a scalloped device popularised by custom painters.

1970 T120RT

Only close inspection would reveal that this is not simply a standard 1970 T120R in US-market trim, externally very similar to the 1969 Bonnie but sporting the following year's Astral Red and silver colours. The engine number's T suffix and some small casting details on the cylinder barrel identify it as a T120RT, a special 750cc version of the Bonneville released on to the American market in small numbers.

In May 1970, favoured dealers across the US were told that they would be allocated an experimental 750cc model as a market-test for a possible future machine of that size, although the real reason for its appearance was to homologate a 750cc Triumph twin engine for racing. Track results were important for sustaining sales against other makes.

The American Motorcyclist Association (AMA), governing body of US sport, had traditionally handicapped overhead-valve engines in road racing and flat track events. They were restricted to 500cc while side-valve machines, in effect the native Harley-Davidson V-twins, could be of up to 750cc.

After joining the AMA as corporate members, the BSA/Triumph organisation pressed for rule changes. Eventually, the archaic capacity limits were abandoned to allow in all types of 750cc engines, for oval track racing in 1969 and road racing from the following year.

In 1969 Triumph had at its disposal the new three-cylinder Trident engine, with 58bhp available in standard form. But while the triple engine would prove excellent for tarmac racing, its bulk and lack of low-rpm grunt meant that it struggled against Harley-Davidsons on the mile and half-mile ovals. Meriden's 650cc twin, with its central crankshaft flywheel and strong torque, was a better tool for the job, but suffered from a 100cc handicap.

Technical staff at Triumph's eastern headquarters in Baltimore came up with an idea for homologating a 750cc twin without waiting for Meriden to produce one. New-season 1970 Bonnevilles had their cylinders and pistons replaced with aftermarket big-bore (3in/76.2mm) kits produced by Maryland-based drag racer Sonny Routt. He agreed to have a batch of castings made closer in appearance to Triumph's than his regular product and to supply high compression (10.5:1) forged pistons. All the components involved were given Triumph part numbers.

The T120RT has a cubic capacity of 748cc, thanks to a Routt big-bore cylinder and piston kit fitted after arrival in the US. Otherwise this machine is identical to a standard T120R for 1970.

When you reach 80mph, the speedometer needle is only halfway round its dial. While gaining some mph, the extra 100cc's biggest benefit is in torque and tractability.

158

After testing prototypes, Baltimore staff rebuilt 145 engines, and another 55 were converted at Triumph's western headquarters in California. A 'T' was stamped on the end of the engine number to identify them. With the 200 needed for homologation produced, the 748cc T120RT gained AMA homologation.

Dealers selling the RT were asked to perform the normal free 500-miles service for customers, followed by cautious service checks at intervals of 1,500, 3,000 and 6,000 miles.

The general run of 1970 Bonnevilles incorporated several changes from the previous year apart from the paint scheme. The most radical in the engine was a revision of the crankcase-breathing facility, previously provided by a timed disc valve at the drive-side end of the inlet camshaft. On 650cc engines from 1970 to the end of production in 1973, three small holes in the crankcase wall vent into the primary chaincase as well as governing the level of oil for the chain. A breather tube from the upper rear face of the chaincase leads to the air filter. Devised by Meriden's experimental department for racing, the system tends to cause condensation, which makes oil in the case milky and may even rust the chain.

The oil tank was enlarged from 5.5 (Imperial) pints to 6 pints, camshaft threads were changed to UNF under BSA's on-going process and the dual seat's base shape altered, resulting in a slight reduction of the seat's overall height.

The 1970 edition is now regarded as the last of the really classic Bonnevilles, a reflection of the widespread disapproval that met the redesign of cycle parts for 1971. Riders can have plenty of fun on post-1970 650cc machines, but many restorers and collectors still shun them.

The 750cc RT version has an additional rarity factor and represents an interesting facet of Triumph history. But it is not necessarily greatly prized by collectors, partly because it contains non-Meriden kit parts and also because more recently built machines with period Routt kits have made buyers wary of fakes.

RTs were converted at random as they were uncrated, but in recent years it has been possible to verify genuine machines through a record of their serial numbers held by the AMA Hall of Fame Museum in Pickerington, Ohio.

This superbly restored genuine T120RT, a model little known outside the US, is from the collection of Graham Bowen.

Barrelled pvc handlebar grips with cushioning were fitted to reduce the effects of vibration from 1966.

Tank graphics with a scalloped panel below the badge, as well as above, had appeared during 1969.

Detail changes for 1970 include front engine lugs bolted, rather than welded, to the frame for ease of assembly and handy drain plugs in the carburettor bowls.

Above left: A T suffix is added to the model code stamping on engines converted to 750cc. Standard 12-point nuts, used from 1968, hold down the flange of the US-made cylinder barrel.

Above: Air filters reduce maximum power, but without them airborne dust can cause severe wear in the cylinder bores. Note the sidecar fitting eye, still present on the Bonneville's frame.

The passenger grab rail is now supported by the mudguard loop.
This US machine has been allotted an age-related UK registration.

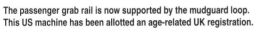

1970 T120RT specifications

Cubic capacity	748cc (76.2x82mm)
Compression ratio	10.5:1
Carburation	Two Amal 30mm Concentric
Ignition	Battery and coil
Charging system	12v alternator
Max power	52bhp (estimated)
Gearbox	Four-speed
Wheels	Front 19in, rear 18in
Brakes	Front 8in sls drum, rear 7in drum
Fuel capacity	2 gal
Weight	365lb (166kg)

1972
T120V
UK SHOW SPECIAL

It may look like a custom job, but this Bonneville T120V acquired its unusually bright finish at the factory. It was prepared by Meriden apprentices for the 1972 Earls Court Motor Cycle Show, where it was raffled to raise money for the Auto Cycle Union Benevolent Fund. Demand was high for tickets costing five pence each and 23,000 were sold before the draw. Peter Worsnop from Wiltshire was the lucky winner and its present owner, Will Holder, bought it in 1976.

The frame is coated with nickel plate and chromium plate is applied to the fuel tank, side panels and other components including the aluminium wheel hubs and brake backplates. The alloy of the outer engine covers is buffed up to a chrome-like finish, while the cylinder barrel and crankcase are painted silver. Emphasising Triumph's nationality, Union flags are prominent on the fuel tank's painted panels.

The eye-catching finish was in the spirit of the times, when Glam Rock was at its height and young bikers loved a bit of extra chrome.

With a nickel-plated frame and various chrome-plated cycle parts, this 1972 Bonneville was specially prepared to be first prize in a charity draw at the 1972 Motor Cycle Show in London.

A similar machine was a lottery prize at the 1973 Amsterdam Show.

Cynics may have suggested that such 'tarting-up' helped distract from negative reaction to the Bonneville's cosmetic makeover for 1971. Common to BSA and Triumph marques, the new look for 650cc twins came from the BSA group's Umberslade Hall R&D facility. It centred

on a duplex frame with a large-diameter spine tube that also served as the oil tank. A sturdy new front fork with alloy sliders pivoted on taper-roller steering-head bearings and protective gaiters for the stanchions gave way to dust seals on top of the sliders. There were 'racer style' conical wheel hubs. The front brake was still an 8in twin-leading-shoe

drum, but the linkage operation was replaced by a 'pull-together' system worked entirely by the cable; the result was disappointing.

Slab-sided panels merged with an air box designed to help meet increasingly stringent noise regulations, the flat-backed headlamp and skimpy front mudguard were supported on wire brackets, and a tapered

megaphone shape was adopted for the silencers.

Production was severely delayed: one snag was that complete Triumph engines could not be assembled into the new frame, meaning that the rocker boxes had to be redesigned. When the 1971 models were eventually released, all but the tallest riders found the seat excessively high, a fault highlighted

by pre-production testers but not acted upon. A reduction in oil capacity meant that engines tended to run hot and the benefit of direction indicators was partially negated by poorly designed Lucas handlebar switchgear. However, for all its faults, the new frame handled well and seat height was reduced by 1 1/2in on the lowered 1972 version that would see out the Bonneville's production life at Meriden.

At the same Earls Court Show where this bike was displayed, Triumph unveiled the latest stage in the Bonneville's evolution.

Responding to American pleading, a 750cc version coded T140V would be available from 1973. The larger engine had a new cylinder head, now with a tenth bolt near the centre and a cylinder barrel with 75mm bores, increased by another 1mm early in production. Its connecting rods and cylinder barrel were shorter and cam profiles were devised to give the strongest power at relatively low rpm, to avoid overloading the crankshaft main bearings. The primary chain was now a triplex type. Changes shared with the 650cc twin included a hydraulic

disc front brake plus a race-bred five-speed gearbox signified by a V (a Roman '5') in the model code.

Not long after the 750cc Bonneville reached showrooms, dire financial problems caused the whole BSA empire to collapse. As motorcycles were a vital dollar earner for Britain, the government organised a rescue under which the smaller Norton Villiers group, maker of the 750cc Norton Commando, took control of Triumph during 1973 and the BSA motorcycle brand was allowed to die.

Norton Villiers Triumph, as the new grouping was called,

announced that it would close Meriden and move Triumph twin production to the bigger but older BSA plant in Birmingham. The workforce were appalled and, rallied by trades union leaders, a significant number occupied and blockaded the factory in the autumn of 1973. After 18 months of bitter dispute, the incoming Labour government supported a workers' co-operative that aimed to keep the factory up and running, and in the summer of 1975 the Meriden Co-operative began assembly of an updated 750cc T140 Bonneville for the 1976 model year.

Triumph's six-fifties were restyled for 1971, with cycle parts designed outside the Meriden factory. Megaphone-shaped silencers and conical wheel hubs were meant to create a racer look. Direction indicators were a standard fitment from 1971.

The new-look front fork, modelled on the Ceriani racing type, has small pvc dust seals instead of gaiters. The new front brake has twin-leading-shoe operation without a rod linkage but does not improve on the earlier design in service.

Far left: The Show Special's UK market four-gallon fuel tank is chrome-plated and carries patriotic Union Jack graphics.

Above: Flat-sided air boxes and side panels were a feature of the 1971 facelift. Normally in a single colour, here they have a non-standard scheme.

Left: Five-speed gearbox internals, a spin-off from factory racing development, were an optional extra introduced for 1972. From 1973, all T140s were five-speeders.

A twin-downtube frame with engine oil carried in its main spine tube was a major part of the 1971 redesign. It caused serious production difficulties and made for a very high seat, lowered by 1972. The flat-backed headlamp and its wire stays were not well received.

This one-off edition has had only two owners and is happily preserved in its original trim.

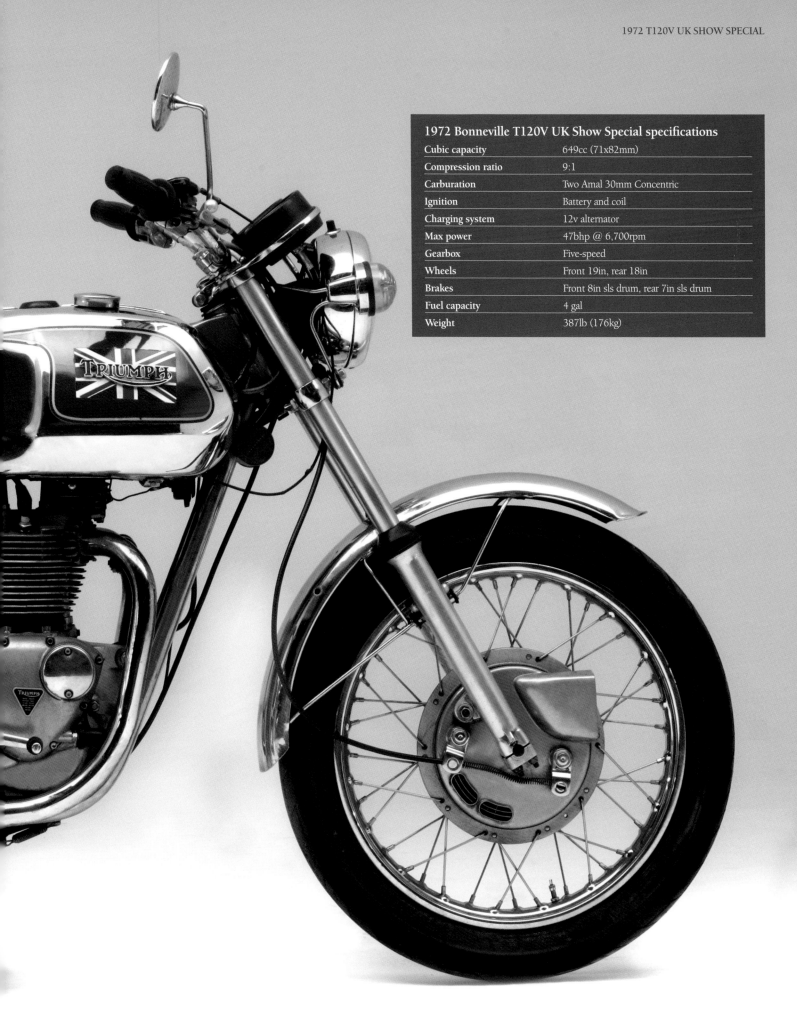

1972 Bonneville T120V UK Show Special specifications

Cubic capacity	649cc (71x82mm)
Compression ratio	9:1
Carburation	Two Amal 30mm Concentric
Ignition	Battery and coil
Charging system	12v alternator
Max power	47bhp @ 6,700rpm
Gearbox	Five-speed
Wheels	Front 19in, rear 18in
Brakes	Front 8in sls drum, rear 7in sls drum
Fuel capacity	4 gal
Weight	387lb (176kg)

1977
T140J
JUBILEE

The special-finish 750cc Jubilee Bonneville of 1977 was an early example of the limited-edition motorcycles that enjoyed a vogue in the late Seventies.

By the late Seventies, the high-performance motorcycle market once ruled by the Bonneville had changed drastically. Japan's four biggest manufacturers were vying with each other to offer ever more advanced large-capacity machines, while European makers BMW, Ducati, Laverda and Moto Guzzi also had strong superbike contenders. Reviewing the T140V, the American magazine *Cycle* called it the 'Nostalgia Express'.

Emerging from a deep crisis, the workers' co-operative running Triumph with government support was not able to compete on technical specification or sheer performance, but hit on an imaginative marketing ploy for 1977. In that year festivities were taking place around Britain to celebrate the 25th anniversary of Queen Elizabeth II's accession to the throne, and Triumph decided to mark the occasion by releasing a limited edition of 750cc Bonneville T140s with a special Silver Jubilee finish. The original idea is credited to Bill Morgan, part of a management team from the GEC industrial giant, seconded to Meriden as advisers.

The red, white and blue of the United Kingdom flag was added to the silver base colour, bright chrome plate was applied to the outer engine covers, and a re-shaped dual seat was covered in royal blue vinyl with red piping. Pin-striping incorporated in the paint scheme exploited under-used skills possessed by some

The royal red, white and blue paint scheme
was applied by factory staff with coach-
lining skills. A flexible bung on the tank
top covers a recess for the fixing bolt and
carries a special badge on the Jubilee.

Co-operative members and extended to the wheel rims, where enamel was applied for the first time in the Bonneville's production life.

The T140J Jubilee was issued in UK and US variants, the latter having, of course, higher handlebars and a smaller, rounded fuel tank without knee-rubbers. Originally 1,000 of each version were produced and sold with a certificate of authenticity, but strong demand from other markets had to be met by issuing a further 400 examples.

Many dealers allocated a single T140J kept it as a showroom display machine or as a souvenir of golden years with Triumph that now seemed in jeopardy. For private buyers, it was often the exclusivity and collectability of the Jubilee that secured a sale. Many of those surviving today have led a sheltered life, some being kept purely for ornament.

This Jubilee is a perfect example, having less than 10 miles recorded on its odometer. Third owner Ray Twiss, a motor trader who owns other classic and modern Triumphs, bought it because he'd always wanted a Bonneville and needed a machine that did not need restoration work before being ridden. But he then decided that once put on the road, his Jubilee would lose its exclusivity.

Such careful preservation has ensured that clean examples of the T140J survive, as the special finish has tarnished on many machines used in all weathers. The bright plating applied on aluminium engine castings is particularly vulnerable and peeling chrome is also a problem.

The Jubilee edition attracted

The master cylinder for the disc front brake, fitted from 1973, is on the right handlebar. The ignition switch is easily accessed on the left-side headlamp bracket.

wide publicity and must be one of the best known of the Bonnevilles among the public at large. Tribute was paid to it in 2002 when the present-day Triumph company offered a modern version to mark the 50th year of the Queen's reign.

For Triumph the sales of 2,400 Jubilees was a significant boost during a tough period. The workers' blockade of 1973–75 had completely halted production, starting a long and bitter dispute with brand owners Norton Villiers Triumph, with the government in the middle. Many hoped that the Meriden Co-operative could succeed, but its future looked uncertain.

Union leaders had mooted forming the workers' co-operative, not so much out of socialist idealism, but as the only way that the Bonneville could be kept in production at Meriden, saving as many of the 1,500 jeopardised jobs as possible. American dealers, represented by Bob Myers of Free State Cycle in Maryland, lent their support. After a change of government early in 1974, the incoming Labour administration made it a reality. Cash was provided to buy equipment and rights from NVT, who would handle distribution.

The relaunched 1976 T140 had a left-side gear pedal and a disc rear brake. The relocated gearchange was mandatory for standardisation with the US market, where it had been deemed that a motorcycle's brake pedal had to be operated by the left foot.

The exigencies of survival meant that the 650cc Bonneville had to be dropped, once remaining 1974 models were completed and despatched. NVT's own motorcycle factory closed down in 1975, and in 1977 the co-operative took charge of its own distribution and marketing. The Seventies ended on a promising note for the Co-op. In 1979, the Bonneville topped the UK's 750cc market with 37 per cent of sales and readers of *Motor Cycle News* voted it Machine of the Year.

Three warning lights and a lighting switch are housed in the full-depth headlamp shell.
The blue and white logo on the speedometer face is that of NVT, who handled distribution
and sales of Meriden Co-operative-built machines from 1975 to 1977.

The carburettors have extended float tickler buttons for easier access and the air lever is mounted adjacent to the left-side instrument.

Left-foot gearchange, mandatory in the US, was adopted for the 1976 model year. Chrome plate applied to the aluminium primary chaincase is vulnerable to weathering.

Releasing the special edition T140J was a successful venture that shifted 2,400 units and helped the precarious Co-operative. A high proportion of machines were saved as souvenirs, like this virtually unused example.

1977 T140 Jubilee specifications

Cubic capacity	744cc (76x82mm)
Compression ratio	7.9:1
Carburation	Two Amal 30mm Concentric
Ignition	Battery and coil
Charging system	12v alternator
Max power	50bhp @ 6,500rpm
Gearbox	Five-speed
Wheels	Front 19in, rear 18in
Brakes	Front 10in disc, rear 10in disc
Fuel capacity	4 gal
Weight	413lb (187kg)

1982
T140LE
ROYAL

Five years on from the Jubilee Bonneville, Triumph released another limited-edition machine. It was timed to celebrate another royal occasion receiving massive pre-publicity in Britain: the wedding of the Prince of Wales, heir to the British throne, and Lady Diana Spencer in July 1981. Again, there were alternative versions for the home and US markets, this time with more marked cosmetic differences.

This is the American variant of the Bonneville T140LE Royal, albeit an example that was re-routed on to the UK market and bought by Midlander Andy Ball. He found it in October 1982 at LB Motorcycles in Coventry. Formerly Len Bayliss Motorcycles, the shop was moving over to motocross machines and keen to shift old stock. Andy paid £225 extra for the American-made Morris cast aluminium wheels that were normal wear on two other Triumphs at the time – the touring-equipped Executive and the US custom-style T140D Bonneville Special. The latter had previously sported Lester cast wheels, also US-made, from a batch that the Co-operative obtained at a good price but that eventually ran out.

The first chrome-plated fuel tank seen on a production Bonneville is a distinctive feature of the Royal, with the usual rounded shape for the US. The style of tank-side emblem first seen in 1970 was revived to make its final appearance, this time with blue lettering on a plated ground. A badge on the tank-top bolt cover carries the three-feathers symbol of the Prince of Wales.

Paint on the US Royal is a rich smoke-effect blue with scalloped

This **T140 Royal** is the US version, purchased through a UK dealer and now restored. The owner, who had it from new and used it in all weathers for some years, has removed the indicators and electric starter, also changing the front mudguard for a T140D item.

Scalloped paint scheme is applied over chrome plate on the US-type three-gallon tank. From 1978, rubber sound-dampers were threaded through holes in the fins on each side of the cylinder head.

Royal Wedding 1981

panels on the tank edged with gold pin-stripes. The seat design is strongly influenced by the 'king and queen' type, a popular aftermarket product in America. The stepped form, with clearly defined rider and passenger positions, is accentuated by grey panels on the vinyl cover.

Extra shine on the US Royal includes a highly polished finish for the front fork sliders, outer engine covers and instrument binnacles. Triumph began using French-made Veglia speedometers and rev-counters from 1978, as supplies of Smiths instruments dwindled and then dried up altogether. Rear-view mirrors, which Triumph were slow to adopt as standard fittings despite their contribution to safety, are provided.

Girling, suppliers of rear suspension struts to Triumph since before the Bonneville was born, had stopped making motorcycle units so Triumph gradually switched to Marzocchi products. The Italian units fitted to the Royals have 'piggy-back' damping fluid reservoirs.

The home-market Royal had Meriden's latest Italian-made four-gallon fuel tank with plain Triumph logo badges. Paintwork was black, except on the frame, which was silver; this was the first frame on a standard Bonneville not to be enamelled black. Black finish was also applied to the engine, the front fork sliders and the headlamp, matched by a plain black seat cover. Production of T140LE Royal machines was limited to 250 units, split between the US and UK types. Like the Jubilee, each came with a certificate of authenticity.

Significant changes had been made to the T140 power unit since 1977. The Bonneville's trademark splayed intakes had been replaced by parallel inlets when Amal Concentric MkII carburettors were adopted, originally on machines shipped to the US in 1978. The change was forced by anti-emissions legislation, which included a ban on the fuel spillage caused when the MkI's float bowl 'tickler' was used for cold starting. MkIIs had a lever-operated choking device and Amal worked with Meriden Co-operative technicians to obtain emissions acceptable to the EPA (Environmental Protection Agency), the resulting machine being coded T140E. The side panels were reshaped to suit and the main engine breather was vented into the air box to recirculate fumes and oil mist.

From 1979, an electronic ignition system developed by Lucas replaced the contact breaker points with a control box behind the right-side

American made seven-spoke Morris cast wheels, also fitted to other T140 variants from 1982, were an optional fitment on this Royal.

panel and a simple trigger unit in the former points location. The change ended fiddly maintenance and ensured single-kick starts. Another advantage of points-less ignition is that spark timing can be perfectly synchronised between the two cylinders, making for smoother running.

As bought, this bike was equipped with Bing constant-vacuum carburettors. Appearing on Co-op machines from 1980 as supplies from Amal became irregular, the German-made instruments with 32mm chokes are of higher quality but give a less crisp throttle response. Andy replaced them with Amal MkIIs, purely because he prefers their appearance. For the same reason he removed the unsatisfactory electric starter fitted to several T140 variants from 1980, replacing the bulky timing cover needed to enclose its drive mechanism. Also, the direction indicators were removed and the original front mudguard swapped for a shorter T140D item.

Sculpting of the seat-top is influenced by aftermarket 'king and queen' seats popular in the US.

A carrier plate integral with the left fork leg supports the Lockheed front brake caliper. Early disc systems often had plain rotors without perforations to help clear rainwater.

Limited-edition credentials are included on the vehicle identification plate riveted to the steering head gusset. This is US build 34.

Above: The cylinder head introduced from
1978 has parallel inlet tracts, placing the
carburettors closer together with a compact
air filter box. Amal Concentric instruments
were used from 1978, although this 1981
machine originally had Bings.

Made in England transfers on frame
downtubes emphasised the Bonneville's
heritage at a time when Japanese machines
had come to dominate world markets.

Left: Rear brakes catch the worst of the
water and dirt. The caliper has a chrome
cover and a plastic gaiter fits over the
hydraulic hose. The rear suspension units
are Italian.

The finned inspection cap on the timing cover gives access to the electronic ignition's trigger unit in the former contact breaker location. Smoke-effect paint seen on the side panel appropriately adds a touch of class.

The **T140LE** is rarely seen today and the **royal marriage** it celebrated would turn **out** to be ill-starred.

1982 T140LE Royal specifications

Cubic capacity	649cc (71x82mm)
Compression ratio	8.5:1
Carburation	Two Amal 32mm Concentric MkII
Ignition	Lucas electronic
Charging system	12v alternator
Max power	50bhp @ 6,500rpm
Gearbox	Four-speed
Wheels	Front 19in, rear 18in
Brakes	Front 254mm disc, rear 254mm disc
Fuel capacity	3 gal
Weight	410lb (186kg)

1983
T140WAV TSS

This is a really rare late Meriden machine. Powered by the eight-valve version of the T140 engine, it features Triumph's AV (anti-vibration) frame that never reached commercial production. The one-off built in January 1983 is owned by London-based Triumph fan Erum Waheed and is in regular use.

The eight-valve TSS engine addressed an issue that had dogged Triumph ever since the resumption of production in 1975. How could the ageing Triumph twin engine hold its own against more technically advanced superbikes while complying with stricter emissions regulations?

Development was overseen by former Triumph Engineering draughtsman Brian Jones, who had joined the Co-operative as engineering manager in 1977. He was impressed by the power boost given by an eight-valve top-end kit for Triumph engines made by Weslake. Founded by carburation and combustion specialist Harry Weslake, the Sussex-based company counted the Gurney Eagle Formula 1 car's 48-valve V12 engine and a winning four-valve Speedway engine among its achievements.

Weslake's 686cc kit was originally supplied to the public via Rickman Motorcycles in the late Sixties, but later became available direct from the maker. Paired valves, with a narrower included angle than Triumph's, were operated from the four pushrods by forked rockers.

Meriden's ultimate development of the 750cc Triumph twin has four valves per cylinder, electric starting and anti-vibration engine mountings.

The TSS wasn't Triumph's first multi-valver: an admired 500cc single with a four-valve cylinder head designed by Ricardo Engineering had been built at the old Coventry factory from 1923 to 1927. At that time four-valve heads were as much about improved reliability and economy as the enhanced performance that Meriden sought.

In 1976 Weslake sold the rights to its Triumph kit, and a complete engine developed from it, to Nourish Racing Engines. NRE provided Meriden with a kit to suit the T140 engine in 1979

and subsequently hired tooling to the factory.

Jones made changes to the NRE design, including more Triumph-like fin shapes, stub-mounted carburettors and cast-in rocker pedestals. Early batches of heads, cylinder barrels and rocker boxes were cast in aluminium by Weslake before Triumph switched the work to Copal Castings in Birmingham.

Meriden engineer Martyn Roberts designed a stiffer crankshaft to cope with higher rpm. Machined all over, it had larger crankpins and narrower big-end bearings, with the connecting rods offset to suit wider spacing between the bores. Pre-production engines went to Big D Cycle in Dallas, Texas, where Jack Wilson of 1956 Bonneville fame ran them in twin-cylinder class racing. His 750cc eight-valver was timed at 153mph on the Daytona Speedway.

The production engine was first seen in public at a show in April 1981, hidden inside a radically styled prototype with comprehensive fairings, designated TS-8, that also debuted the AV frame.

There was little enthusiasm for the TS-8, but when the TSS was released with a normal T140 frame in 1982 (as a 1983 model) press testers praised its mid-range grunt and found vibration much less intrusive than with the two-valve engine. The weekly *Motor Cycle News* quoted top speed as 122mph.

Nearly 440 TSS models were made. While NRE's kit was reliable, Triumph's adaptation of it had many faults, oil leaks being the least bad.

The AV frame derived from the Co-op's desire to pick up police fleet contracts. In earlier times Triumph had been proud to be a leading supplier of machines to forces in the UK and abroad. But as time went on potential buyers were concerned about engine vibration damaging radio equipment and causing rider discomfort. Most

Although quoted peak power of 59bhp came at 6,500rpm, the TSS engine could withstand higher revs than the 8,000rpm maximum indicated on the Vegila rev-counter.

forces favoured BMW's smooth flat-twins.

A crankshaft balancer device developed at Meriden tempted at least one police force, but the cost of making the entirely new crankcases needed was prohibitive.

Enter Bernard Hooper Engineering. Fourteen years earlier Hooper had been in the team behind the Norton Commando with its Isolastic frame that mounted the entire power train on flexible bushes. His company prototyped a Meriden twin with a more refined flexible mounting system to discover that it was remarkably smooth.

Hooper licensed Triumph to use the system and John Rosamond, chairman of the Meriden Co-operative at the time, recalls that nearly 50 AV frames were built, individually by hand as there was no production tooling. A few police-specification AV machines were assembled with two-valve engines.

The problem then was not in persuading police forces to buy, but being able to deliver fleet orders with BMW-type reliability from a shrinking factory with a permanent cash shortage.

Originally a police model, this machine was restored in civilian trim by Reg Allen Motorcycles in West London. Proud owner Erum says the superior performance and smooth ride make it the ultimate Meriden Bonneville.

Triumph reshaped the finning on the NRE/Weslake cylinder head. Internal modifications caused problems, including oil build-up resulting in leaks.

PORTRAIT OF A LEGEND

On this machine, the rider's footrests are set slightly further back than on other T140s of the period.

These seven-spoke alloy wheels look like Morris products, but were made as samples for Triumph by the Japanese Ensu company, now known as Enkei.

The eight-valve engine gives a boost of
nearly 10bhp without added external bulk.
Few seven-fifties of the early Eighties were
so slim.

The crankcase is finished in black, as are the cylinder and head, with their fin-edges left in natural aluminium silver.

The rearward-mounted footrest requires a remote linkage for the gearchange lever.

Unobtrusive anti-vibration engine mountings make this TSS even smoother than the standard model on the road.

Closure of the Meriden factory in 1983 cut short development of a Triumph twin with great potential for speed and comfort.

1983 T140W AV TSS specifications	
Cubic capacity	744cc (76x82mm)
Compression ratio	9.5:1
Carburation	Two Amal 34mm Concentric MkII
Ignition	Lucas electronic
Max power	58bhp @ 6,500rpm
Gearbox	Five-speed
Wheels	Front 18in, rear 18in
Brakes	Front twin 254mm discs, rear 254mm disc
Fuel capacity	4 gal
Weight	423lb (192kg)

1983
T140ES
TSX

'A YAMAKAWAHONZUKI IT AIN'T' shouted Triumph's advertisements promoting the TSX in the American motorcycle press during 1982. Meriden's latest restyling exercise was aimed at spirited young American riders who didn't want to follow the herd by choosing a bland Japanese machine. Not necessarily seeking

extreme performance, they wanted something that could hold its own pulling away from traffic lights, was easy to handle and looked cool.

A similar idea had been tried in 1979 with the Bonneville D Special, also aimed at younger US customers. Failing to make a big impact, it was scuppered by a sudden rise of the dollar against the pound.

Early in 1980 Meriden's chief engineer, Brian Jones, proposed a 'Semi Chopper Project' inspired by Monaco Cycle Sales in Franklin, Pennsylvania. A flourishing Triumph dealer since 1964, John Monaco had no qualms about modifying machines with aftermarket parts to suit customers' preferences – even before they hit the showroom floor. The favoured

style was the 'low-rider' look, fashionable in urban America.

To control costs, Jones didn't want to deviate far from the T140E Bonneville base but his proposals included seat, handlebar and foot-peg positioning to follow the US fashion for 'low riders'. He envisaged a 16in rear wheel, stepped seat and short megaphone-shaped silencers, suggesting that if

such a model was ready by 1981 it could exploit a market trend with a possible showroom life of three years. A Triumph Low Rider was displayed at the 1980 London Motor Cycle Show, but purely as a concept machine.

The prime mover behind getting the custom-style TSX into production was Wayne Moulton. He had been appointed in 1980 to run Triumph Motorcycles America (TMA), the company set up three years earlier by the Meriden Co-op to market its products in the US. Previously with Kawasaki America, Moulton knew the market well and had conceived the successful LTD custom variants of existing Kawasaki models. He had a prototype assembled, which Meriden followed faithfully.

Using the basic T140 as a platform, Triumph Motorcycles America created the striking TSX custom-style variant.

The TSX shares the engine of the T140ES electric-start Bonneville available from mid-1980. Located behind the cylinders, the Lucas starter motor turns the crankshaft via a lengthy train of reduction gears and a sprag-clutch, tucked inside a bulging timing cover. Push-button starting had been the norm on motorcycles for years, so it had to be added. But even Co-op experimental department technician John Hallard, who was involved in making it work, has never believed it a satisfactory arrangement.

The cylinder head and rocker boxes are black, with their fin edges picked out in bare metal, as had previously been seen on the UK edition of the 1981 T140LE Royal. The distinctive exhaust system has large-diameter downpipes without a bridging tube and tapered megaphone-style silencers reminiscent of the 1971–72 type. The carburettors are 32mm CV Bings.

The cycle parts make the TSX stand out from other models in the range. The wheels are US-made Morris alloy castings with a slim 3.25 profile tyre on the normally sized 19in seven-spoke front rim and a chubby 4.50-section cover on the small-diameter 16in rear wheel. To accommodate the rear tyre, the swinging arm is specific to this model and the engine unit shifted slightly to the right to achieve the necessary chain line. The seat is stepped, although the rider's portion, at 30in, is not drastically low.

Shaped to suit the carburettors, the moulded side panels blend with the fuel tank, unique to the TSX with its single tap and external balancer tube. Other Italian-made fitments are the eye-catching Paoli rear shock absorbers and the Brembo rear brake.

Applying graphic devices to the fuel tank and side panels was a new departure for Triumph. Their striped motifs look equally attractive with both the Gypsy Red base colour on this example and the lesser-seen black option. Had production not terminated early in 1983, a TSX-8 variant powered by the eight-valve TSS engine was slated for 1984.

Records show that 381 TSX models were built. This one was sold on the UK market in early 1983 and is equipped with the optional kick-start lever. Its sixth owner is Erum Waheed for whom a restoration to original condition was carried out by Reg Allen Motorcycles.

The TSX, and especially the TSS with its potentially strong performance, demonstrated the Meriden Co-operative's determination to win through. But it was too late and, despite loans and export credits, a chronic lack of money meant that the end of the road was reached early in 1983, when the last machines came off the Meriden line.

Specially made for the TSX, the tank has a tube underneath to balance the fuel level between the two sides.

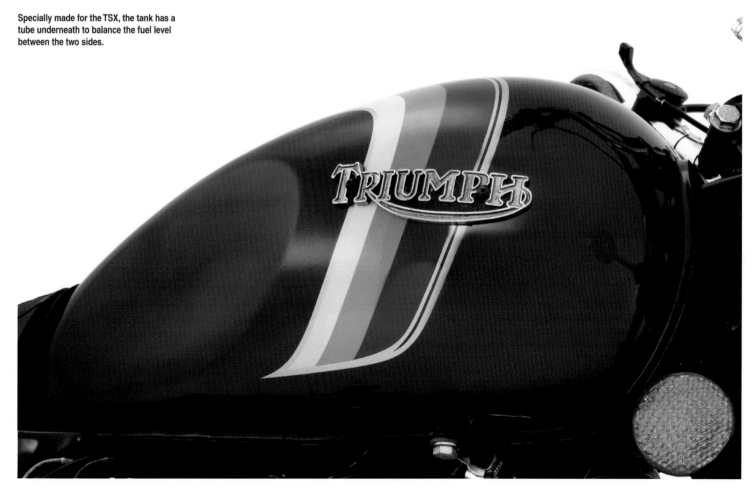

A fascia for the ignition switch and warning lights sits between the Veglia instruments. This assembly was fitted to T140s from 1979. Multicoloured tank graphics were novel for Triumph.

Above: The TSX was one of the twins fitted with 32mm Bing CV carburettors instead of the traditional Amal type.

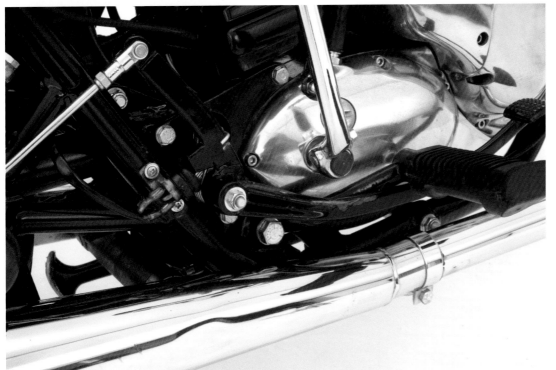

Far left: A pronounced bulge on the timing cover encloses the electric starter's chain of drive gears.

Left: The rear brake pedal is linked to the master cylinder by a rod, with a rubber-shrouded stop light switch fixed to the frame.

The chubby rear Avon tyre on a 16in rim
is a key element of the custom look.
The rear brake caliper was sourced from
Brembo in Italy.

Alloy wheels are by Morris, front brake caliper by AP Lockheed.

1983 T140ES TSX specifications

Cubic capacity	744cc (76x82mm)
Compression ratio	8:1
Carburation	Two 32mm Bing
Ignition	Lucas electronic
Charging system	12v alternator
Max power	49bhp @ 6,500rpm
Gearbox	Five-speed
Wheels	Front 19in, rear 16in
Brakes	Front 250mm disc, rear 250mm disc
Fuel capacity	2.8 gal (Imp)
Weight	420lb (190kg)

1988
LF HARRIS
BONNEVILLE

Little more than two years after the Meriden factory closed for good, the Bonneville was back. Its reappearance came about thanks to the tenacity of Les Harris, owner of LF Harris (Rushden) Ltd, a British motorcycle parts supply company based in Newton Abbot, Devon.

Londoner Harris had been a BSA-mounted teenaged tearaway before joining the motorcycle trade. He built up his business both by manufacturing pattern parts for popular models and by buying masses of disposal stock during the British industry's decline, not always at knock-down prices. Harris was branded a 'parts pirate' by some, but the Meriden Co-operative helped his business by abandoning 650cc spares supply and the role he played in keeping obsolete British machines on the road for their proud owners is undeniable.

Harris was unsuccessful in bidding for rights to the Triumph brand when it was sold by the West Midlands Enterprise Board in 1984, but he did acquire some factory jigs and tooling for the T140. Overall marque rights were bought by John Bloor, owner of a successful Midlands-based house-building company and a life-long Triumph admirer.

Bloor had ambitious long-term plans, but needed a few years to develop thoroughly up-to-date products. In the meantime, his privately owned Triumph

The revived Bonneville assembled at a small plant in Devon is very close in specification to the machine Meriden had planned for 1984.

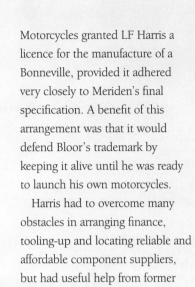

Motorcycles granted LF Harris a licence for the manufacture of a Bonneville, provided it adhered very closely to Meriden's final specification. A benefit of this arrangement was that it would defend Bloor's trademark by keeping it alive until he was ready to launch his own motorcycles.

Harris had to overcome many obstacles in arranging finance, tooling-up and locating reliable and affordable component suppliers, but had useful help from former Triumph draughtsman Brian Jones and other ex-factory personnel.

In mid-1985 the 'Harris Bonneville' was unveiled, attracting considerable interest from both the specialist and general media. Mr Harris, who drove a Rolls-Royce, would be praised for his enterprise by Prime Minister Margaret Thatcher and invited to the Tokyo motorcycle show.

Anyone who naively expected an all-British product from LF Harris had to accept that building such a motorcycle was no longer a practical possibility. However, most engine components were manufactured by UK contractors, using more modern precision machinery than had been available at Meriden. The crankshaft was a modified version of the admirable TSS component, but terms laid down by Bloor prevented it having the four-valve engine's stouter crankpins.

As on all pre-1981 Bonnevilles, carburation was by Amal, although

its Concentric instrument was by now made in Spain. A rubber-mounted type based on the MkI, but with a cold-start setting instead of a float tickler, was manufactured specifically for the revived T140.

Before closure, Meriden had begun procuring an increasing number of components from the healthy Italian motorcycle industry, which supplied Paoli front forks and rear shocks, Brembo brakes and LaFranconi silencers as well as fuel tanks. German parts included the Magura handlebar controls and brake master cylinders, while the French Veglia company supplied

instruments as it had to Meriden. A battery by leading Japanese brand Yuasa was specified.

There were hiccups. Bloor rejected the first machine submitted for quality evaluation, and a damning 'road test' – by a German journalist who didn't know he was riding a factory hack with a tired Meriden engine – did some damage. But in the first press test of a new machine by *Classic Bike* magazine early in 1986, a top speed of 115mph – a creditable figure for a resurrected 'oldie' – was recorded at the MIRA proving grounds.

Harris produced a total of 1,246 750cc twins, some being single-carburettor TR7 Trophies for the Royal Signals White Helmets display team. Bonnevilles were sold in the UK, Europe and the Antipodes, a very few with electric starting. Under the licensing terms, none was officially exported to the USA, where product liability complications threatened. Production in Newton Abbot ended when the licence agreement expired in 1988. Les Harris died in 2009 but spares for Meriden Triumph twins are still produced by the company, now trading as LF

Harris International.

The machine seen here is owned by David Drew, who bought it from London dealer Roebuck Motorcycles in 1988. He saw it as a last chance to own the new Bonneville he had always craved since his youth. David paid extra for the aftermarket Norman Hyde oil cooler, fitted stainless steel braided brake hoses and painted the rear sprocket non-standard black. The only problem encountered in several thousand miles was a leak from the exhaust rocker box spindle that was repaired under warranty.

Above: Tidy modern switchgear and easily adjusted rear-view mirrors are among attractive practical details.

Left: The Italian-made fuel tank conforms to the traditional US-market shape and uses the familiar scalloped paint scheme.

In this case Made in England is stretching the point, as many cycle parts are of foreign manufacture.

Side panels follow a style seen in product leaflets Triumph prepared for the 1984 season. Like the majority of Harris machines, this example does not have electric starting.

A non-standard accessory, the Hyde oil cooler between the frame downtubes is inconspicuous.

1988 LF Harris Bonneville specifications	
Cubic capacity	744cc (76x82mm)
Compression ratio	7.9:1
Carburation	Two Amal 30mm Concentric Mk1.5
Ignition	Lucas electronic
Electrical system	12v alternator
Max power	50bhp @ 6,500rpm
Gearbox	Five-speed
Wheels	Front 19in, rear 18in
Brakes	Front twin 250mm discs, rear 250mm disc
Fuel capacity	2.4 gal
Weight	440lb (196kg)

Above: Speedometer and rev-counter are from Veglia, previously a supplier to Meriden.

Left: Brembo brake calipers and Paioli fork legs contribute Italian flavouring to the British beef.

2010
BONNEVILLE
SIXTY

After several years of preparation in tight secrecy, John Bloor's Triumph Motorcycles launched its range late in 1990. A complete break had been made with the past and even the Triumph logo was subtly changed. Manufacturing had been set up in a freshly built factory on the Leicestershire/ Warwickshire border near Hinckley.

Starting out with a range of large-capacity models with three-

and four-cylinder double-overhead camshaft engines, the reborn Triumph company intended to be world-class, as Meriden had been in its heyday. Within five years production had exceeded 12,000 machines a year as Bloor focused on Triumph's return to the US. Old model names were resurrected for modern designs, but Hinckley's fastest superbike was called the Daytona and not the Bonneville.

The hallowed name was reserved

for a model more likely to be ridden by riders who remembered Meriden Bonnevilles. In 1997 work began on a moderately powered machine that would appeal to both entry-level motorcyclists and mature riders, including 'born-again bikers'. At the time there was a growing market for 'naked' unfaired motorcycles with retro styling.

Revealed for 2001, the first Triumph Bonneville to be available for 12 years turned out to be an air-

cooled twin-carburettor 360-degree parallel twin. But that was as far as the internal engineering went in resembling the old twins.

Originally 790cc and later enlarged to 865cc, the Hinckley engine's horizontally split crankcase supports a crankshaft with four half-circle bobweights on plain main bearings. Two balancer shafts placed ahead of and behind the crankshaft, are driven off it by gears and ensure a smooth ride.

Looks familiar! Triumph set out to make a modern twin cylinder machine, while keeping close ties with the style of the pre-1983 Bonnevilles.

There are four valves per cylinder and drive to the double overhead camshafts is by chain from the centre of the shaft with gear distribution at the upper sprocket. With two trochoidal pumps, the wet-sump lubrication system plays a part in engine cooling. Primary drive to the five-speed gearbox is by gears and final drive is on the right side of the machine. Naturally electric starting is standard.

Outwardly, the engine faintly echoes the Turner twin. The valve gear sits deep in the top end to avoid excessive height, the cylinder finning and outer engine covers hint at the old style, while a breather at the front of the barrel is wittily made to look like one of Turner's pushrod tubes.

When European emissions rules forced a change from carburettors to electronic fuel injection for 2008, injector bodies that kept the appearance of the previous

carburettors were commissioned from Keihin.

Overall machine style is keyed to the Meriden look. A teardrop fuel tank, separate headlamp, side panels and spoked wheels are all redolent of the late Sixties' T120. The only elements that seem to jar with Meriden Triumph fans are the ridged lower edge of the tank and kinks in the exhaust pipes ahead of the silencers. The latter were necessary to gain cornering clearance for angles of bank possible on modern tyres.

Although odd in appearance where it is strongly reinforced behind

the steering head, the tubular duplex frame provides exemplary handling. Understandably, disc brakes are fitted.

This example is the 2010 Bonneville Sixty, with a 1960 T120 colour scheme. The lighter shade is now called Meriden Blue while the darker is Caspian Blue, and a hand-painted gold lining divides them. Since the original 2001 version, many variations have been played on the basic theme, including the America introduced in 2002 and offering an alternative engine form with a 270-degree crankshaft to mimic the lolloping gait of a V-twin.

The centenary of Triumph motorcycles in 2002 was marred by a catastrophic factory fire in the main Hinckley plant, but reconstruction was achieved with miraculous speed and full production resumed within six months.

In 2004, another evocative name from Meriden days was revived when the Thruxton hit the streets. For those who found the standard 61bhp 790cc Bonneville a little too docile, it offered extra speed and torque from the bigger 69bhp 865cc engine and a sportier riding position to match. Two years later came another interesting variant,

the 54bhp Scrambler with an eye-grabbing high-level exhaust system.

There is no doubt that the latter-day Bonneville lives up to the legend – and the expectations of 21st-century owners. The engine is bullet-proof in its standard forms, Triumph paintwork is known for durability and, after some past problems, nuts and bolts with exceptional resistance to corrosion are used. While fairly weighty and by no means a speed machine by today's standards, the twin has sold strongly at home and abroad, helping Hinckley exceed the entire output of Meriden.

Ergonomic and attractive handlebar switchgear is far removed from the equipment Triumph had to settle for 40 years earlier.

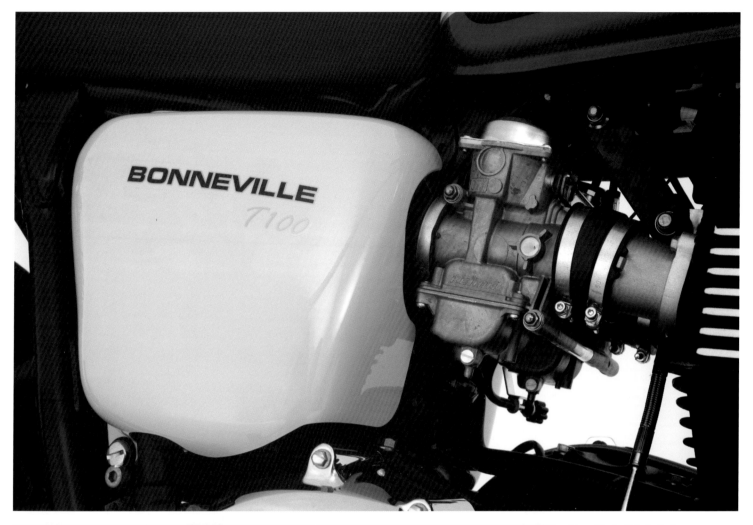

Above: The fuel injector bodies, necessary to meet emissions regulations, are cunningly disguised as carburettors.

Far left: The timing cover and gearbox outer casing evoke classic shapes designed by Edward Turner.

Left: Shades of late Meriden: fin edges are picked out against the black base colour of the cylinder head. Engine oil plays a part in cooling.

Reliable, well-finished and with enough power to exceed 100mph, the 21st-century Bonneville has proved popular in its various guises. This edition has a colour scheme like that of the 1960 T120.

The Hinckley factory has its own logo, but its swooping R that joins to the H evokes the original.

2010 Bonneville Sixty specifications

Cubic capacity	865cc (90x68mm)
Compression ratio	9.2:1
Fuel system	Keihin EFI
Ignition	Lucas electronic
Max power	66bhp @ 7,500rpm
Gearbox	Five-speed
Wheels	Front 19in, rear 17in
Brakes	Front 310mm disc, rear 255mm disc
Fuel capacity	3.5 gal (Imp)
Weight	507lb (230kg)

JAMES MANN

MICK DUCKWORTH

James Mann is a dyed-in-the-wool automotive nut.

As well as photographing for over 40 car books and five bike titles including Original Bonneville, he has owned a succession of motorbikes over thirty years, his current machine being a 1965 Triumph T100SC.

His work regularly appears within the pages of numerous magazines all over the world and James is as happy on location as he is in the studio – but prefers the studio when it is raining.

He has visited the Bonneville Salt Flats to see where the magic all began, but chooses to live in Dorset with his wife and two children. www.jamesmann.com

Mick Duckworth started riding motorcycles as a teenager in the Sixties, riding well-worn machines across fields in his native Isle of Man.

His love of two-wheelers led to him writing about them and the opportunity to join the staff of *Classic Bike* magazine in 1983 provided contact with the worldwide classic motorcycling scene as well as training in journalism.

A freelancer since 1994, Mick has specialized in historic subjects, regularly visiting the United States. He lives in Nottingham with his wife and a small collection of motorcycles, some of them functioning.